S0-AQI-692

# Expressions of Aging

## By John Keston

### With Richard A. Lovett

42K Books
Champaign, Illinois

**Library of Congress Cataloging-in-Publication Data**

Keston, John, 1924-
    Expressions of Aging / by John Keston ; with Richard A. Lovett.
        p. cm.
    1. Keston, John, 1924- 2. Long-distance runners--United
States--Biography. 3. Actors--United States--Biography. 4. Running for
older people--United States. I. Lovett, Richard A. II. Title.
    GV1061.15.K47K47 2011
    796.42092--dc22
    [B]

                            2011002490

ISBN: 978-0-615-44684-4
Copyright © 2011 by John Keston

All rights reserved. The publisher takes no responsibility for the use of any of the materials or methods described in this book, nor for the products thereof. No part of this book may be reproduced in any form or by any means without permission from the author.

Published by 42K Books, a division of 42K(+) Press, Inc.
Printed in the United States of America.

Questions regarding the content of this book should be addressed to
42K Books
Attn: Jan Seeley
206 N. Randolph, Suite 400
Champaign, IL 61820
217-359-9345

Cover photo: John Keston, on a run, and as famous 17th-century biographer John
    Aubrey (whom he portrayed in his one-man show, "Expressions of Aging")
Editor and project manager: Jan Colarusso Seeley
Cover photo/design: Ryan Brennecke
Interior design and layout: Judy Henderson
Copyeditor: Dick Lipsey
Proofreader: Ray Vallese
Printed by: Premier Print Group
All photos courtesy of John Keston.

# The Seven Ages of Man

*by William Shakespeare*

All the world's a stage,
And all the men and women merely players;
They have their exits and their entrances,
And one man in his time plays many parts,
His acts being seven ages. At first the infant,
Mewling and puking in the nurse's arms.
Then the whining schoolboy, with his satchel
And shining morning face, creeping like snail
Unwillingly to school. And then the lover,
Sighing like furnace, with a woeful ballad
Made to his mistress' eyebrow. Then a soldier,
Full of strange oaths and bearded like the pard,
Jealous in honor, sudden and quick in quarrel,
Seeking the bubble reputation
Even in the cannon's mouth. And then the justice,
In fair round belly with good capon lined,
With eyes severe and beard of formal cut,
Full of wise saws and modern instances;
And so he plays his part. The sixth age shifts
Into the lean and slippered pantaloon,
With spectacles on nose and pouch on side;
His youthful hose, well saved, a world too wide
For his shrunk shank, and his big manly voice,
Turning again toward childish treble, pipes
And whistles in his sound. Last scene of all,
That ends this strange eventful history,
Is second childishness and mere oblivion,
Sans teeth, sans eyes, sans taste, sans everything.

*As You Like It*, act 2, scene 7

To Anne—J.K.

To the runners, especially the Duniway Lizards.
You know who you are.—R.A.L.

# CONTENTS

# FOREWORD

## 80 Years . . . and Counting

When I was young, I was fascinated by old people. As a child, I could listen endlessly as they recounted stories of lives and times far before mine. The older they were, the better, because each decade added extra mystery to the stories they brought to life. Later, as an actor, I was always irked by performers who portrayed old people with strange mannerisms and quivery voices. These weren't the old people I knew: the ones I knew had too much of life still in them.

Aging, for those of us fortunate to live long enough, is inevitable. As a friend of my coauthor, Rick Lovett, likes to say, "Consider the alternative." We cannot escape it, so the best solution is to enjoy the process of getting there. The most beautiful old people I've met have made no bones about aging. My mother-in-law, Alma Norton, aged graciously all the time I knew her—still enjoying herself until she died at 104.

Throughout my life, older folks—and runners—have always played an important role. Intriguingly, many of the older folks came early in my life; the runners (generally younger than I) came later.

I would never have been the person I am without Alfredo Morelli, my voice teacher in Naples, Italy, or Caligaris, whose generosity and concern for a young English singer was unbounded. Nor would I ever have made my mark in theater without T. Armon Jones, a wonderful 83-year-old baritone who could still pop off some stunning high notes, or Harold Miller, who during some of my leanest years gave me voice lessons free of charge. Also vital to my development were my father and mother, who gave me moral support when times were hard, always confident that I would eventually have the theatrical career I so much desired. Then there was Sir John Gielgud, who saw potential in a nervous young actor's reading for Noel Coward's *Private Lives* and engaged me to understudy the leading role of Elyot, in London's

West End theater district. Many other older people have passed through my life and disappeared into the mists of time. But their marks remain. Highest on that list are the wonderful retirees from Denver who overheard me singing and who worked tirelessly to ensure my initiation to America.

Nor can I omit my dear families and all the young friends of my life. They have all played parts in my development as an artist and world-champion runner, and I continue to treasure them as they too "grow old along with me," knowing, like the poet Browning, that "the best is yet to be."

It has been an adventure all the way. There is much to be thankful for and little to regret. As Samuel Ullman recommends:

> Live with Enthusiasm. Youth is not a time of life. It's a state of mind . . . . Nobody grows old by merely living a number of years. People grow old only by deserting their ideals. Years wrinkle the skin, but to give up enthusiasm wrinkles the soul.

All of these people have helped the development of my own philosophy of life, which can be summarized in seven words: be kind to everyone, and keep moving.

Finally, I am grateful for the encouragement to set out my story. Specifically, I thank Rich Benyo, Joe Henderson, Roger Robinson, John Stanton, and all the others whose good company I have enjoyed at racing events around the United States, Europe, and Canada. Rich and Roger, great storytellers both, are the single strongest inspirations for this book. Sharing my own stories with them, I found them listening to me as I had listened to the older people of my youth. "You've got to write a book, John," they said, and at long last I have.

# Once a Runner— Always an Athlete

## McMinnville, Oregon—1997

"Phew! Eight minutes, 45 seconds," I said. "Not too bad." I was running, if that was an even remotely appropriate word, loops of the driveway circling my mother-in-law's apartment complex. *Lurching* was probably more like it.

Only eight days earlier, I had broken my hip in a bicycling accident. It's amazing how fast such things can happen: an angling railroad track, a moment's inattention, and *bang* I was on my side, knowing it would be a while before life returned to normal. Maybe that is why I'm a runner more than a cyclist. Bicycle racers break bones. Runners try very hard not to.

In the emergency room, the doctors told me what I feared: I had broken my hip and would need major surgical repairs as soon as possible.

Seconds before the crash, I had been a world-class runner who, at age 73, had several world records to his credit and was hoping for more. Now, I was . . . yes, *lurching* was indeed the right word . . . through these quarter-mile loops, in times not wildly different from those I had once posted for entire 3,000-meter races. Well, maybe a bit different. My best 3,000 had been 10:51, when I was 70. My 8:45 quarter mile had beaten that by a tidy two minutes and six seconds. Still, I was hobbling along on crutches at a pace more suitable for the snail Olympics than a world record.

If there was a single trait that had characterized the first 73 years of my life, it was what the English call "sheer cussed-mindedness." Before I had taken up running at age 55, that trait had led me to considerable success as a musical comedy actor, opera singer, and stage performer, though it had taken the first 38 years of my life for that stubbornness to finally bear fruit. Running was simply the same thing: if you worked at something hard and long enough, you could do more than you thought.

A week after my bike crash, the computer game *Riven* would be released. In it, I played the pivotal role of Gehn—a villain who pops up in several key scenes for those who get far enough into the game to begin working out its final puzzles. And earlier that year, a week after the filming of *Riven*, I had seen one of the greatest triumphs of my running career.

Gehn is an old man. I was now old by most people's definition. But from the moment I started running, growing old had become fun. Each year, I had felt not only stronger but physically and mentally more able. Even my theatrical work had become more dynamic and more rewarding. My mind seemed keener and more agile, and I had even become better, in middle age, at teaching next year's generation of youngsters. More than just infusing my life, running had invigorated it.

Then had come *Riven*—and a week later, one of the best races of my life. The two halves of my personality had finally come together.

Now, though, I simply wanted to get around this dirt track faster than 8:45. The key was to improve my . . . what would you call it? . . . *crutch* turnover? In running, it would be leg turnover, but this form of locomotion was a bit different.

The orthopedic bad news had been accompanied by good; it was a clean break. With the repair, I could hope for a full recovery. So, one day after the accident, I let the surgeons insert a pin into the femur, securing it with screws. Twenty-four hours later, I was allowed to hobble around the nurses' station on a walker. A few hours after that, I graduated to crutches. Now, I was trying to find out what I could actually do with these infernal contraptions.

My second lap was 26 seconds faster, an 8:19. Hurrah, a new record! I wasn't breathing any harder than the first time, nor had the physical effort seemed noticeably more difficult. *I could definitely go faster on the third loop*, I thought.

• • •

Following the surgery, e-mails flowed in from throughout the running world.

From Mike Tymn, running legend, author, and regular contributor to *Runner's World* and *National Masters News*:

John, very sorry to hear of your accident, although I don't believe in accidents, per se. Everything happens for a purpose; there is a lesson to be learned. I suspect you will come out of it even stronger than before.

From Dr. Hal Goforth, exercise physiologist to the U.S. Department of the Navy:

I'm convinced that the level of injuries is always a constant so that when one person is injured another can be well; so I thank you in that respect. I am sure at some time in the future I can repay you by being injured when you are running well.

From John Stanton and friends at the Running Room, with several stores throughout Canada and the United States:

I agree with your doc. Many high-performance athletes have been forced to rest and then return to a higher level of performance on their return. Now is the time to write. You should share your story.

Jerry Crockett of USA Track & Field phoned to add that 17 years before, he had had a similar bicycle accident, breaking both hips and requiring many more pins and plates than I did. Recovery took a year and a half, he said, but afterward, he collected several U.S. records for his age group.

All of my doctors and physical therapists concurred. Because of my pre-accident fitness, I could look forward to full recovery. There was no reason I couldn't regain my former racing prowess. What I did with that would, of course, be up to me.

• • •

I wasn't halfway through lap three when a whistle and shout stopped me dead in my tracks.

"What the heck have you been up to?" a high-pitched voice called from behind. It was male, and while I had never heard him sing, I presumed that if he did, he would be a tenor, like me—though you can never be sure from speaking voices. My own stage voice is a resonant baritone, but it hides operatic highs.

The speaker was a man of about my age, coming toward me in bare feet, a concerned look on his face. "John, how can it be that you're already out and about?"

I assured him that I had full medical approval (although I secretly doubted that a timed speed workout was what the doctors had in mind). Still, it was easy to convince Ken that I knew what I was doing. An American of Welsh descent, he was proud of his heritage and found a common bond in my own English roots—and as a fellow septuagenarian, he was extremely proud of my athletic accomplishments. "Keep up the good work," he said, and padded back to his apartment. Later, I saw him watching from the window and suspected that he might be giving his wife a running commentary on my progress.

Happy to give him a good show, I finished my interrupted lap and then prepared for one final effort. *This is it*, I thought. *This one's definitely going to be faster*. I would love to say I really was getting stronger, but I'm sure it was more a matter of learning to use the crutches. Still, I made it in 6:56, a definite PR! If it really was a quarter mile, I had finally gotten my pace up to better than two miles an hour—27:44 per mile, to be precise. And that had been despite several interruptions to laugh. Only a runner would try to run laps on crutches! Only a serious competitive runner would time them! Still, I knew that what I was doing would pay off in the long run.

Then I proved that even on crutches, "sheer cussed-mindedness" still dominated my spirit. Even though I had already nearly tripled the longest distance I had yet done on crutches, I was thinking of doing it one more time. After all, it's the last one that really counts. It's the last one that gives you the biggest bang for your training buck.

I rested briefly and then pushed the button on my watch and was off again: Ken undoubtedly thought I was insane. The entire neighborhood probably agreed. Not that it bothered me: I'm a runner and actor—being thought insane goes with the territory.

There is a rhythm to running on crutches, and I was finally beginning to find it. The last lap sailed by . . . no, that's not the word, but it will do . . . in six minutes, 40 seconds. A new record, if only by 16 seconds. Time to call it a day. I had hobbled now, for one and one-quarter miles, at times reaching the spectacular rate of 2.5 miles an hour. Later, as my wife was changing the dressing on my incision, I was gratified to see that the staples were intact. Training hard was one thing. Setting myself back was another, though I was resigned to the fact that I might do it occasionally. It's part of what "sheer cussed-mindedness" means.

Cussed-mindedness is one of several traits that unite my running life with my theatrical life, but it is only now, from the vantage of my 86th birthday, that I realize how strongly these two portions of my life mirror each other. In many ways, it's as though I've lived two parallel lives, one beginning when I first laced up running shoes in 1980s Minnesota, and the other much earlier, in Europe.

# First Strides

## *T*oo Poor for Underpants—England 1924–39

*"Yeah, we know, Dad. When you were a kid, your family was so poor you didn't have underpants." John shook his head at me, mocking.*

*"Ha, ha, ha, and you lived in a big cardboard box and ate only carrots," Richard chided.*

*It was the mid-1970s and I was no longer poor, but I had just told my sons that, at the moment, I couldn't afford to buy them new hockey skates. I had then launched one of those unfortunate phrases parents realize they've overused only when their kids preempt the story by tossing it back to them: "When I was a kid . . ."*

*But the truth was that there was an era when I was too poor for underpants, though I had a perfectly good home and ate plenty of food other than carrots.*

• • •

I was born Francis Douglas Arthur Caston in Paddington, London, on December 5, 1924. Francis was my father, Douglas an uncle. I have no idea where the "Arthur" came from.

If there was athletics in my ancestry, I didn't know of it. But theater ran in my blood. My parents were good but untrained singers who regularly participated in amateur concerts and revues. One of my grandmothers had been a vaudeville singer; the other was a classical singer and pianist who had performed for Queen Victoria. But the most intriguing was my paternal grandfather, who was a "top-boot dancer"—a lost predecessor of tap dancing done in long-footed boots that are alternately slapped on the stage or balanced on their skinny, extended toes.

The "perfect" distance runner is thin, wiry, and not exceptionally tall. As a child, I was two of the three. I would ultimately grow to well above average height, but not all great distance runners are short.

In the early 1980s, when I belatedly took up running, Alberto Salazar was setting the marathoning world afire, and he was five feet eleven and 144 pounds. I gave up one inch to him in height but was only four pounds heavier: a perfect build, it would turn out, both for running and the types of theater roles that most appealed to me.

Like many who grew up poor but well loved, I remember my childhood as carefree and happy. I would have preferred to have had underpants, but my school shorts were made of gray flannel and lined so that they were reasonably comfortable, and the omission was less a hardship than one might imagine.

Dad worked nights as a supervisor at a London telephone exchange. It sounds like an important position, but it didn't pay well, and working at night meant he had to sleep during the day. That must have been tough on him with four children in the house, but once my sisters (one older, two younger) and I were in school, his sleep was rarely disturbed except at lunchtime, when giggles might erupt into guffaws so raucous that Mum would have to shove us out the back door into the garden to quiet down.

Impatient with the time it took to walk to and from school, I would run as much as possible. By the time I was 12 or 13, I was running the entire double round trip—five miles a day, five days a week. Today, you read about Kenyan superstars who did the same as children, but at the time, my running career lay 42 years in the future.

Lunch breaks lasted an hour and a half. Except when giggles intervened, my sisters and I helped Mum with her work, which involved tying ribbons onto greeting cards. Every day, the lunch table would be laden with cards for whatever holiday loomed next: Christmas, Easter, Valentine's Day—or perennial favorites such as birthday cards, wedding cards, or congratulatory messages of other sorts. The pay wasn't much, but for a family of six, it was a much-needed supplement. My sisters and I would set up an assembly line in which some would fold cards while others threaded ribbon through holes in their edges. We would then pass the cards to Mum, who would deftly tie pretty bows to complete them.

It was a lot of work for little pay, and sometimes it was obvious that my parents couldn't meet their bills. At those times, a knock at the door would be greeted with a request for me to peek out the window to see if it was the insurance agent who came weekly to collect petty premiums for whatever ills that my parents were insured against. If it was, I would signal my family, then my mother and sisters would hide under the table while I huddled beneath the window until he was gone. I suspect he received far worse treatment from other families. From us, he usually got his premiums on time, and missed ones were always made up.

If money was particularly short, the rent collector might receive the same treatment. But as kids, we never seemed to view these fiscal events as serious crises. Often, hiding from view threatened to unleash one of our giggling fits, and we would almost suffocate—inspiring, of course, yet greater urges to giggle—by stuffing anything and everything into our mouths to keep silent until the peril had passed.

As I got older, Mum sometimes allowed me to answer the door. In my most solemn, young-gentleman manner, I would then inform the bill collector that she was out and not expected back until late evening and that sorry, she hadn't left the payment.

All told, life was good. We were a loving family, and Mother never complained or even seemed disappointed at not having greater material goods. Just as running to and from school was preparing me for life as an athlete, pulling off those little prevarications with the bill collector was teaching me the rudiments of acting. Before entering either career, however, I would first lie about my age and go through a preliminary career as an airplane mechanic.

## Bemidji State University, Bemidji, Minnesota—1975

"Oof," I said—*rather pointedly*, I thought. But my racquetball partner never noticed. He was a big bruiser, perhaps one hundred pounds heavier than me, and supercompetitive.

I had recently moved to Minnesota for what I thought would be a one-year teaching position. Instead, it would prove to be one of the most important transitions in my life, marking the end of my full-time acting career and setting the stage for my life as a runner. Indirectly, my racquetball partner would prove to be one of the more important links in that transition.

I had no problem with his competitiveness; I can be that way myself. But he kept slamming me into walls to block my shots, and that *hurt*. Worse, racquetball wasn't even my game. *My* game was squash. It's an elegant game, played with a racket the size of a ping-pong paddle on a stick, a bit like a badminton racket, but sturdier. The ball is similar to a racquetball ball, but smaller and less bouncy, and the game is played in a room somewhat like a racquetball court, though it doesn't work in a racquetball court (I've tried).

Squash is a game for people who like to run for the ball and hit it hard, because that low-bounce ball won't go anywhere if you don't. Racquetball is more a game of reflexes and court sense; if you position yourself correctly, that bouncy ball will come to you, rather than your having to go to it. What this means is that while a good game of racquetball is a decent workout, an enthusiastic game of squash is a *great* workout.

I had taken up squash a decade earlier in London as a way to work off job stress. But here, the university didn't have even a single squash court. For a while, I tried to teach the game to other faculty members, playing it against a wall in the gym. But we were missing the flavor of the real thing, where the ball bounces all over the court at odd angles. We were also spending too much time retrieving balls from the far end of the gym, where they inevitably wound up when you missed a shot.

And so, I had reluctantly taken up racquetball, only to find myself covered with purple welts from all the times that superfast ball kissed you (a squash ball doesn't hit that hard!) and regularly getting the breath knocked out of me by one of the few opponents whose schedule matched mine.

My new job had the advantage of being much lower stress than what I was used to. That meant that while I missed playing squash, I no longer felt as much need for it, or any sport. I had always before been active, but never in any systematic way, and now, at age 52, I gradually let it slide. If I didn't like racquetball, why play? It was another of those critical turning points whose significance you don't see until later. Ironically, the act of getting badly out of shape would be what led me to the sport for which my body was best suited.

## Not Good Enough for the Choir—London, 1932

As a child, I loved listening to music on the radio. Every evening, starting at 5 P.M., Henry Hall and his Dance Band came on BBC radio for an hour. Each day I stopped whatever else I was doing to listen. It didn't take long until I had memorized everything they had ever done, practicing around the house when nobody else was listening.

My elementary school had a choir, and I thought it might be fun to sing with them. In today's world, any child who wants to sing is allowed to do so, but the only way into this school's choir was by audition.

Had I been allowed to perform Henry Hall's songs, I probably would have passed the audition with flying colors. But the school choir director picked the music—just a few phrases, identical for each child. Then, one at a time, we were called to stand in front of her. It was supposed to be like being on stage, but without the support of the choir it was far more intimidating.

I was only seven or eight and lacked the musical background to understand precisely what went wrong. Perhaps the music was unsuited to my voice. Perhaps the superformal audition setting scared me so badly I couldn't produce enough volume. Whatever the cause, I do remember the outcome. "I'm sorry," the teacher said, "but I don't think you have a voice. I'm afraid I can't have you in my choir."

My parents were supportive. "Try again some other time," they said. But I was crushed. When I again took a formal interest in art, in my teens, my interest then was painting. I was good at it, good enough that some of my paintings hung on my school walls for many years, good enough to win a scholarship to an art school. But secretly, I continued to sing.

## Natural Healing: Bemidji State University, Bemidji, Minnesota—1980

By 1980, my physical conditioning had been declining for several years, but I barely noticed it. I was still thin and fit looking and thought I was healthy.

Then one day I took a free blood-pressure test. The result was distressing: 150/85—high enough to warrant attention. As soon as possible, I was in the doctor's office for a more thorough exam. "We need to check your kidneys, too," he said, informing me that high blood pressure can damage them.

I allowed myself to be X-rayed, and shortly the doctor was back, showing me shadowy outlines on a sheet of photographic film.

"That's a cyst on your kidney," he said. "It's got to be the size of a cantaloupe. I've never seen anything like it before."

I felt like the freak of the week, but of course there was a more urgent concern. "Is it cancer?"

"I don't know. To be honest, it's fifty-fifty."

It was the day before a holiday weekend—Easter perhaps—and I spent a fearful three days waiting to be admitted to the hospital for further tests. There, they inserted one needle into me to drain a liter of fluid from the cyst, followed by another that inflated it like a beach ball to provide better contrast for another round of X-rays. "Good news," the doctor finally said. "It's something we call a smooth-walled cyst. Definitely not cancer."

Relief flowed through me. For three days, I had wondered whether I even wanted to know the outcome of the test. Now I felt like a condemned man who had just gotten a reprieve. But there was still the original problem. "Did the high blood pressure cause it?"

"Maybe. Maybe not. Either way, we need to do something about it. If we don't, eventually it will give you problems."

We discussed the options, among which low-salt diets and blood-pressure medications featured prominently. But while doctors, hospitals, and medications have their place, they're rarely my first choice. Years later, when I broke my hip falling from my bicycle, it took some effort for my doctor to talk me into getting it pinned. Left to my own devices, I would have preferred to go home and wait for nature to fix it her own way. For the hip, that would have been a serious mistake. For blood pressure, nature does have a good solution: exercise.

If I couldn't play squash and didn't like racquetball, I would have to find something else.

## Anderson Shelters: London—1939–41

*The bomb exploded like muffled thunder. High explosive, not an incendiary, an analytical corner of my mind recorded. You can tell the difference because HE goes "boom," while incendiaries pop and sizzle. It was also close—close enough to shake the ground beneath my feet, close enough, in fact, to blow in part of the front wall of the home where I had once hidden, giggling, from bill collectors.*

*It was perhaps the closest I have yet come to death. The bomb fell across the street from our house, killing two people and converting several homes into a deep crater. But I was 15 and thought I was immortal. London during the Blitz was merely one big adventure in which I hoped to make a heroic mark, doing my bit to beat back the Nazis.*

• • •

I was still a schoolboy, well shy of 15 when the war broke out. I hurried to finish school, graduating at 14 1/2. My next step would have been art school, and whether I would then have wound up a painter, I will never know. With the Germans rampaging across Europe, studying art seemed a selfish thing to do, especially when everyone I knew was employed in the war effort, one way or another. Besides, being paid an adult wage was itself appealing, so I passed up the scholarship and took a job in a factory that made airplane cowlings and fuselages. It was difficult work, but that didn't bother me: I still had enough energy to bicycle to work, using the suction behind the double-decker buses to race through the four-mile commute.

Even during a war, there is need for relaxation. In fact, the need is probably more critical than in normal life. On weekends, briefly setting aside the very real worry that our country might soon fall to the Nazis, friends and I would bicycle 40 miles to visit the beaches of Brighton. There, we would swim and eat enormous dishes of ice cream before turning around to pedal back another 40 miles before dark. It would establish in me a lifelong practice of using exercise to burn off stress—yet another habit that helped set the stage for my eventual conversion to an athlete.

We lived in Morden, a suburb on London's south side. When the German planes attacked London, they frequently flew over us, en route to their targets. If they were turned back before reaching their primary goals, they would drop their bombs on us before making their escape back across the Channel. At first, the planes came only at night, and the targets were airfields and factories such as mine, which made military equipment. But soon, the raids shifted to a generalized assault on the British populace—a pounding that continued day and night. I can remember being on my bicycle as the bombers roared in low, not much higher than the rooftops. I should have been terrified, but I merely gaped, foolishly confident that of all the millions of people in England, I wasn't their target.

The daylight raids were bold, but sometimes they cost the Germans dearly. I will never forget the elation I felt one morning when I read in the paper that our boys had blown three hundred planes out of the sky in a single day. By the time the bomb fell on our neighbor's house, the raids had shifted back to nighttime only, and amazingly, people were beginning to take it as part of their routine. Each evening, after Dad left for work, my mother made sure the blackout curtains were drawn, so no hint of light could help German pilots find their way. Then we would wait for the air raid sirens, which would give us 15 to 20 minutes' advance notice when German planes were heard coming in from the coast. And come they did, night after night after night. Sometimes we sought refuge in subway stations, which were so deep beneath the surface that you could sleep undisturbed, completely unaware of what was happening above. More often, we slept in our own Anderson shelter.

Early in the Blitz, the government realized that people were Britain's single greatest asset. Hitler was trying to destroy our morale and demolish our workforce, and one of the best ways to defeat both of those goals—not to mention protecting everyone's friends and families—was with a construct known as the Anderson shelter.

I don't know who Anderson was, but he probably saved more lives than anyone else in World War II. The shelter was built of six arched pieces of corrugated iron that bolted together to form a mini-Quonset hut large enough to house a dozen people in reasonable comfort. To erect it, you dug a hole in your backyard, at least four feet deep, and assembled the shelter inside it. Then you covered the top and sides with sandbags, creating a remarkably sturdy bunker. The floor didn't even get muddy in the rain. The government gave us the materials, but we had to do the work—not a disagreeable task for an energetic teenager accustomed to factory work. When it was finished, I felt perfectly safe inside—and if my mother and sisters disagreed, they chose not to voice it. My father was usually at work, but some nights he joined us.

On the night when the bomb fell across the street, we were all safely inside, along with the residents of the house that had taken the brunt of the blow. Another family from one of the destroyed buildings had taken refuge in another Anderson shelter that wound up practically on the edge of the crater, and they too survived.

The two people who died were from a family that stubbornly decided not to abandon their home. I felt sorry for them, but one of the tragedies of war is the way it numbs you to the many lesser tragedies of which it is comprised. Twenty to thirty thousand Londoners died in the Blitz. My neighbors were two of them. Another aspect of war is that, in some ways, I feel that tragedy more strongly now than I did at that time.

Not all air raids were spent in the Anderson shelter. Not only did we sometimes seek the quieter, more sleep-conducive shelter of the Underground, but occasionally, the noise was that of incendiaries, rather than high explosives. On those nights, I wouldn't allow myself to huddle in safety. Incendiary bombs exploded with lesser force than the high-explosive ones, but they scattered sparklerlike devices throughout the neighborhood. If these weren't promptly extinguished, everything wooden would go up in flames.

The government drilled us on the proper protocol for extinguishing an incendiary. A bucket of water would do the trick, but those were rarely handy. Better was to use a sandbag from your shelter.

Extinguishing an incendiary was dangerous because there was no guarantee it wouldn't explode again as you approached it. Sometimes they were designed to do that, in order to scatter the burning flares more widely, increasing the damage. These explosions weren't large by the standards of the one that converted the homes across the street into a gigantic crater, but neither were they anything you wanted to be close to. Proper technique was to carry your sandbag in front of you—the bigger the bag, the better—and not to loiter until you had managed to drop it in place. Hitting your target on the first try was also a good idea.

I should have been terrified each time I did this, but I was young, naive, and jacked up so high on adrenaline that I never noticed. There would be plenty of times in later life when I would run races in pretty much the same state of mind, but at least then, the consequences of failure would be considerably less alarming.

## Bemidji State University—1980

It was the height of America's first running boom—the heady years from 1972 through 1984, when familiar names like Frank Shorter, Bill Rodgers, Alberto Salazar, Mary Decker Slaney, and Joan Benoit Samuelson ranked with the world's elite. Even some Minnesotans made that limelight: Gary Bjorklund, Dick Beardsley, Janis and Barney Klecker.

Bemidji was a logging and paper-mill town of nine thousand people, only one hundred miles from the Canadian border. To the extent it's famous, it's for an enormous statue of Paul Bunyan and his giant blue ox, Babe. But even here, we had some serious runners. Included among them were several of my students. One spring noon, they invited me to join them. We went four or five miles—way too far for a beginner, but I survived and joined them again. Soon we were jogging all over town, chattering about music and history and politics and whatever else crossed our minds in the easy camaraderie of runners everywhere. It never crossed my mind that it was unusual that I, at age 55, had no trouble keeping up. But apparently, they noticed. As spring edged into summer, they urged me to try a local 10-kilometer race.

If they were expecting a tough sell, they didn't get it. My blood pressure was falling nicely, I was enjoying running, and I knew that racing was an important part of their lives. "Sure," I said. "Why not?"

Racing was a new experience. I had run hard on occasions with my students, "burning out the gunk," as subsequent friends have called it. But I had never before exerted myself for 6.2 miles, nor had I done so in a setting where you're actually trying to see what's the best you can do. I loved everything about it: the nervous energy of the start; the mass adrenaline as 180 runners surged forward at the gun; the course, which took a scenic route through the university campus and along the shore of Lake Bemidji. But the biggest surprise was that I won my age division— quite tidily, in fact, with a time of 44:44, or 7:13 per mile. I was lucky, of course, that it was a small race. Where I live now in Oregon, several 55- to 59-year-olds could have bettered that time without breaking a sweat. But in northern Minnesota I would rule the 55–59 division in every race I entered.

It was the win, more than anything else, that hooked me on racing. Running would remain my blood-pressure medication, but racing was my passion. Over the next few years, I kept on racing and winning, but I didn't really know whether I was truly fast or just in a slow group. That answer would eventually come from two men: Jack Moran and Alex Ratelle.

## CHAPTER 2

# Growth and Innocence

## Royal Air Force—1941–46

It was the most beautiful sky I had ever seen—not just blue, but translucent, like crystal. The ocean was similar but deeper, except at the tops of the swells, which lightened to a shade closer to that of the sky. By day, dolphins played in our ship's bow wave, while flying fish skimmed the surface. By night, the wake glowed with an eerie phosphorescence.

It was World War II, and I was somewhere in the warmer reaches of the Atlantic Ocean. My ship, the *Mauritania*, was a converted passenger liner, although with several thousand troops on board, the facilities weren't exactly first class. Nor did anyone but the officers know precisely where we were or where we were going, other than that eventually we would most likely wind up in North Africa. All that the rest of us could do was hope our convoy really did know how to avoid U-boats and try to make rough approximations of our latitude from the motions of the sun and stars.

I was a member of the 603 City of Edinburgh Fighter Squadron, whose pilots had fought with distinction in the air war that was already being referred to as the Battle of Britain. It was about young men like these that Winston Churchill said, "Never was so much owed by so many to so few," and I was proud to be among them.

By the summer of my 16th year, I had tired of working in a factory by day and chasing incendiaries by night. There had to be something more I could do. So I lied about my age and joined the Royal Air Force. What I really wanted was to be a pilot, but the medical exam revealed a predilection toward hernias—a problem not improved by my labors constructing our Anderson shelter and toting sandbags. Throughout childhood, I had known that there was a soft lump that protruded from my lower abdomen and sometimes had to be pushed back into place; now I had a name for it. Eventually, I would have an unpleasant number of hernia operations, but the problem may have saved my life. At the time I enlisted, pilots were so badly needed that they were being sent up with only a few weeks' training. Many died. If not for the hernia, I might have been among them.

Impressed by my background at the aircraft factory, the RAF instead decided to make me a flight mechanic and sent me to school in Wales. It took longer to train a mechanic than a pilot, and by the time I graduated, the Battle of Britain was won and squadrons such as ours were being assigned to other fronts. We would not know it for months to come, but the ship was taking us to South Africa, from whence we would eventually be sent to Egypt to help Montgomery in the desert campaign against Rommel.

We had been steaming south for several weeks when I was summoned to my commanding officer's cabin.

"Caston," he said as I saluted. "I got a message from headquarters saying that you're underage. Just how old are you, anyway?"

I was terrified, but lying to the recruiter was one thing. Lying to my commanding officer was another thing entirely. "Going on eighteen, sir," I said. "My birthday is in December." It was March at the time, but at least I had told the truth.

He digested that for a moment, while I wondered how I would be punished. "It was your mother who told them you were too young," he said eventually. She had done it, apparently, when she learned I was being sent overseas.

"She was told it was too late," he added sternly. "We're not about to turn the convoy around just to take you home to your mum." He paused again, while I stood at attention, sure that something dreadful was about to happen. Then he relaxed and I realized he had been testing me. "Good lad," he said. "You're a true patriot."

And so, the ship plowed south. At the time, I merely thought I was heading off to do my bit to win the war—and in my small way, I was. But I was also about to broaden my horizons in ways that would chart the course of my life for the next 30 years.

## Twin Cities (Non) Marathon: Minneapolis/St. Paul— 1982

By the time I had been running for two or three years, I was beginning to realize I was more than ordinarily good. I was logging only 20 miles a week, but I was winning every race in sight, while steadily improving my 10K time. I broke 44 minutes and then cut that to 43. Other runners were encouraging me to train harder, and I began to wonder what might happen if I took their advice.

What little coaching I obtained came from my sons, John and Richard, who were on the high school track team. Occasionally, they would run with me, sharing tips gleaned from their coach. Good runners, I learned, ran high mileage. I increased to 30 miles a week, then 40, and finally to between 50 and 70. Good runners ran intervals on the track. I did the same, and my 10K times again improved. I broke 43 minutes and eventually cut it to 41:53.

I had now been running for two and one-half years and was beginning to set my sights high. Another Minnesotan, Alex Ratelle, was the top 55- to 59-year-old in America, and I fantasized about unseating him at the toughest distance of all: the marathon. In 1982, the big news on the Minnesota running scene was the creation of a major new race, the Twin Cities Marathon, to be run from downtown Minneapolis to downtown St. Paul. Alex was from the Twin Cities, and I longed to race against him on his home turf. So a few months before my 58th birthday, I worked up the nerve to ring up the race director, Jack Moran. The marathon was rapidly filling, but Jack said there was always room for elites. He had not heard of me, though. Could I tell him more about myself?

When I said I was winning my age group in every race in northern Minnesota and hoping to beat Ratelle, Jack interrupted and asked my 10K time. I told him about the 41:53. Since there was nobody I knew who could run remotely close to that time at my age, I thought it was pretty good. But I can still remember the guffaw that ran down the phone line to Bemidji. "You'll need a lot better 10K time than that to beat Alex," he said. Then he rattled off some rather intimidating stats about Ratelle, chief among which were "consistently below three hours in the marathon" and "well below 40 minutes in the 10K."

I was humiliated. It was like auditioning with high hopes of snagging a role for which you actually had no chance. I had presented myself as good, when actually I wasn't much better than mediocre: good enough for Bemidji, but not for the big time. It would be three years more before I again thought seriously about the marathon.

## Egypt and the Mediterranean—1942–43

After taking nearly two months for a journey that in peacetime would require only 10 days, my ship finally docked in Durban, South Africa. Even that circuitous route had apparently not been quite good enough: the rumor mill said that a couple of ships from our convoy had been lost to U-boats. I had never heard the explosions, but the convoy was so large and spread out it would have been easy to miss. It was a bit unnerving, but it was also a lot like being in London during the Blitz. The bombs fell, and even when they were close, it was always other people who died. This didn't even feel all that close—it was more like reading about last night's bombers in the morning paper.

What felt a lot more real was the unbelievable pleasure of again walking on terra firma. But not for long. All too soon we were aboard ship again, heading up the east side of Africa and through the Suez Canal to Alexandria, Egypt, where our Beaufighter squadron would be stationed for several months before being sent to the western Sahara.

Working for the squadron was a lot like working for the aircraft factory, except that I was living in a military camp, not at home, and my work hours were longer and more erratic. Still, just as I had taken weekend excursions to Brighton, now my mates and I occasionally got leave time to sample the offerings of Alexandria.

Alexandria was a big and wondrously foreign city. But it also did its best to cater to the tastes of the troops guarding it from the Nazis. One simple pleasure that never failed was eating at special armed forces canteens that offered eggs and bacon, a wonderful antidote to the monotonous diet of porridge that passed for breakfast back in camp. But of course, there were also plenty of opportunities for drinking. Those of us who were young were eager to experiment, but the older ones would always look out for us when we had had one too many, and our squadron quickly built up a camaraderie that would persist through all future deployments. Nor was rowdiness our sole interest. We visited pyramids and museums and pondered the many civilizations that, like ours, had ebbed and flowed through this ancient port.

Then one day, I was helping lift a tail wing onto a trestle for repair. We didn't have cranes for jobs like this and were forced to rely on brute strength, recruiting whatever personnel were available at the moment: electricians, armorers, engine and airframe mechanics, and other maintenance crew members. I heaved as hard as I could . . . and a familiar pain seared through my groin.

I was promptly admitted to a military hospital where a naval surgeon performed the first of what have been, to date, eight hernia operations. Of all of those operations, this was the oddest, for it was carried out under a spinal anesthetic that left me conscious and alert throughout.

I'm not sure it's that good a thing to be able to eavesdrop on your surgeon while he's cutting into you. He and his staff were discussing a movie they had seen the night before. I can even recall the title: *The Commandos Strike at Dawn*. The whole affair seemed a tad casual for my taste, making me hope he was truly aware of my belly, lying open beneath his knife. Then he interrupted his patter to ask me to cough—checking his stitching job, I presume. I obliged, then a moment later he asked me to cough again. I'll never know whether it was a two-step procedure or whether the first time he had seen something not to his liking, because he immediately went back to chattering with his colleagues. Then he was finished and I was trundled back to my ward.

At first, my recovery offered a quiet opportunity to write letters home, read, and rest. But a few days later, I got my introduction to the reality of the war. Somewhere offshore, a British naval vessel had been bombed by the Luftwaffe. The casualties flooded not only my hospital but several others, and dozens of sailors filled the long rows of iron beds that comprised my ward. At the far end, a young man groaned and repeatedly asked a nurse if he was going to die. He was far enough away that I never heard her words other than as a soothing murmur. Nor did I ever learn whether he lived or died. He wasn't the only critically wounded man in my ward, and for several days, the doctors and nurses were frantically busy tending to them. Then gradually, things returned to normal. The groans and cries for help diminished. Most of the boys were now on the mend or had been transferred to other wards. But some had died.

I no longer felt immortal, and I kept thinking of the wives and mothers who would soon receive the terrible news. I thought of my own mother, who had tried to keep me in England and would daily be worrying about her only son and wouldn't receive my next letter for months.

# Confidence Game: Bemidji, Minnesota—1983–1984

Had it happened earlier in life, my premature attempt to step into the big time at the Twin Cities Marathon might have been the end of my running career. I later came to know Jack Moran well enough to know that he hadn't meant to put me down. But at the time, that's how it felt. Alex Ratelle was within three months of my age and apparently could run rings around me. Who was I to think I could beat him? Until I had deluded myself with visions of glory, I had simply been a guy who had fun going to races and whose main goal was to keep his blood pressure under control. I might have a modest turn of speed, but I really wasn't all that good.

Long ago, that type of attitude had become almost instinctive. Despite my talents as a singer and actor and my love of being on stage, I had always been shy and nervous among other performers. Even when I was one of the stars of the show, I felt like an impostor, afraid that while I might be able to fool the audience, the other actors would know I was faking it—just as my commanding officer in the RAF had discovered I was faking my age. Only this time there would be no reprieve, because this time I wasn't in the middle of an ocean.

Once I was on stage, I had no problems. Somehow, the stage created an artificial boundary. It wasn't truly me up there; it was someone else—someone I was pretending to be. The difficulty came when the stage was absent. That could be a crippling problem in auditions, but it was also a barrier between me and my fellow performers. Worse, it was a barrier between me and friends who might support me.

When I was a teenager, I used to sing on the commons behind our Morden townhouse—the home that would later be severely damaged by the Nazi bomb. Singing *with* other people was fine, and two of my friends and I had just finished an Andrews Sisters tune when my father walked by. "Was that you singing, Son?" he asked. (He always called me "Son.") "It's very good." He had caught me unawares, and it was one of the few times I was able to sing unselfconsciously in his presence. Subsequently, when I was striving to build a professional career, my parents would be my strongest supporters. "Sing us a song, Son," my father would ask, but I would rarely be able to do it because I felt so terribly inadequate. I have few really deep regrets in my life, but not being able to sing more often for my parents is one of them.

Now, I can sing anytime, anywhere. Thanks to running, I have become much more accepting of who I am and what I can do, unconcerned about what everyone else would say or think. But even at the height of my theatrical success, in the recesses of my soul, I was the schoolboy who had been told he couldn't sing, who had somehow managed to fake his way through it ever since but who knew that somehow, sometime, he would be unmasked. It didn't matter that I knew I had talent and had at times striven fiercely to prove it. It really is amazing how long those childhood traumas can persist, deeply hidden but never quite healing.

• • •

For the next year or two, I set Ratelle and marathons out of my mind. But as I continued running and racing, I realized that my new sport was healing more than my blood pressure. In the next couple of years, I found myself developing a new self-image. With it came the sense that I could tackle anything without fear of failure. That didn't mean I wouldn't fail—just that I didn't need to fear it. After all, not every race is a personal best. You shrug, figure out what went wrong, and focus on the next one.

It took time, but I noticed a similar trend in the theatrical performances that were an adjunct to my teaching job. As my running improved, they became freer and more self-assured, allowing me to give more expansively of my art. It hadn't happened overnight, but no longer did I question whether I was any good at my craft.

Meanwhile, I continued to whittle away at my 10K time. Without really thinking about it, I began training harder, and as my race performances improved, I began to think about trying to lower it to 40 minutes or below. That would show that I was worthy of racing against Ratelle!

In this, I was helped by a runner 20 years younger than I, named Bob Wagner. His wife was a soprano with whom I often sang duets, and our families had become friends. Bob and I often did long runs through the woods and interval workouts on high school or university tracks. In races, he always beat me, but in training he often ran my pace. I thought it was merely that he trained relatively slowly. But actually, I was working hard to match pace with him. He knew my goal and constantly encouraged me, saying I could do it easily.

One fall day, on a pretty country road, he told me that I needed to shorten my stride and increase my leg turnover to a faster cadence. I took the advice to heart and began practicing it. Immediately, I felt faster and lighter on my feet. Other than the advice from my sons, it was perhaps the single most important piece of coaching I have ever received.

Then came winter runs in December and January, the darkest, coldest part of the year. The temperature would dip to minus-30 degrees and stay there for days at a time, forcing me to bundle up with several layers of clothing. In extreme weather like that, a critical survival rule is to start every run into the wind. That way, if you've underdressed, you can turn around and run home with the wind behind you, avoiding frostbite.

Another rule, at least for men, is to stuff a plastic bag into your shorts. Otherwise, you can frostbite your nether regions. I had learned this the hard way several years earlier, when at a 10K cross-country ski race (running has never been my sole sport), I hit the bathroom afterward. As warm urine passed through ice-cold flesh, I experienced a sensation unlike anything I ever wish to encounter again. The moans and screams from neighboring urinals indicated that I was not the only one who had been so afflicted.

Now, running with a scarf covering my mouth, I would head out the door for six to 10 miles. An hour or more later, I would return to peel off layer after layer of clothes stiff with frozen sweat. The most visually dramatic layer was my scarf, which was always laden with a giant icicle three to four inches long and a couple of inches wide.

It was an extreme regimen, but I was determined, and could feel myself improving.

## Soya Links and Bedouins: North Africa—1943

From Alexandria, we went to the Western Desert in Cyrenaica, where Montgomery was pushing Rommel's forces back toward Tripoli. For several weeks, we were stationed at Tobruk, rebuilding a captured German airbase. On the inside wall of one bombed-out building was a German soldier's rendering of a beautiful, sparsely clad woman. It was exceptional, not just because she was beautiful but because the art was amazingly lifelike. Amidst the destruction, the painting was unblemished, and gazing on it touched me with the artist's humanity.

Whatever I had thought when I enlisted, killing other people was something I couldn't reconcile with that shared humanity. Everywhere on the base were signs the Germans were much like us: carrying out the orders of superiors, wanting the fighting to be over, wanting to be back in their own lands. I was fighting for a vital cause, but many times I pondered the obscenity and futility of the killings. Outside the shattered buildings on the base were makeshift graves for German lads whose wives and mothers would have received the same type of telegrams as the British wives and mothers whose boys had died in that hospital in Alexandria.

Life at the base was demanding. The pilots were sent on daily sorties, while we were kept busy maintaining their planes. But there were slack periods in which we could borrow a truck for a quick trip to the beach. The Mediterranean was warmer than the waters of the English Channel at Brighton, and I sometimes did enough swimming to get some true exercise. But mainly, it was our primary chance to bathe ourselves thoroughly, because our base had no showers. The best we could manage in camp were perfunctory washings from five-gallon petrol cans. Cut in half lengthwise, these cans made adequate washbasins. We had also learned to convert them to urinals by slicing them diagonally, standing them on end, and drilling holes in what was now the base. These makeshift creations were wedged into another can, which collected the urine, and were half buried in the sand for stability and to place the entire contraption at the right height. These homemade urinals, dotted around the camp, looked a bit like steel flowers, each with a single large leaf. We called them "desert lilies."

Young Bedouin boys would visit our camp with eggs to sell in exchange for our free issue of cigarettes. These cigarettes came in strange packs—round tins of 50—and were extremely unpleasant. Where the tobacco came from, we didn't know; we thought Rhodesia. None of us liked them, but the Bedouins seemed delighted to get them. At first we felt guilty, foisting off our cheap tobacco on them, but we soon decided that fair exchange was no robbery.

Since Alexandria, we had been back on porridge, but thanks to the Bedouins and the cigarettes, we again had eggs, which we could cook on the Primus stoves a few of our mates had been wise enough to acquire in Alexandria.

On occasion, we even got to eat our eggs with sausage—or at least that's what the RAF called the imitation meat occasionally served to us as a "special treat." Actually they were soya links, which are pseudosausages made of soybeans. There are some tasty soybean products on the market today, but these were reminiscent of soggy brown paper ground up with seasoned soy meal. Once at a squadron meeting, our commanding officer went so far as to apologize for them, but he also told us they were very healthful and encouraged us to continue choking them down. From what I know about soybeans today, he was probably right, but at the time I was more interested in the fact that he seasoned this news by telling us that from now on we would be getting regular rations of beer. Unfortunately, "regular" meant "once every three months."

The first beer came a few days later. We were as delighted to receive it as only soldiers in a desert could be—but our entire ration came to a whopping three bottles each. This was to last three months?

Like the cigarettes and the sausages, it wasn't true beer. It was some synthetic concoction made in Canada by Dow Chemical Company, but it tasted remarkably like real lager. Other than the miserly ration, the main problem was that Cyrenaica is scathingly hot, and we had nothing remotely resembling refrigeration. We tried burying the beer in the sand, but except at night, the desert sands were scorching. Then someone remembered how well the wind, hot as it was, could cool a perspiration-soaked shirt. Would this work for beer? A clever lad put a bottle into a woolen stocking, poured water over it, and hung it from the guy rope of his tent. The rest of us tried it too, adding more water as needed, and by evening we had beer that was at least cool or at British pub temperature.

Another member of the squadron had been a champion ballroom dancer before the war. During slack times, he taught us tango, waltz, fox trot, and quickstep. Someone had managed to bring an old phonograph and records from Alexandria, providing our instructor with authentic music. Gliding across a sand floor in army boots isn't easy, and there was much good-natured humor when the results weren't all that graceful, but ultimately we were good enough for dance contests where the winners were presented the ultimate trophy: a "desert lily" to be planted the next day. By the time we returned to civilization, we were sure we would cut a rug with any date.

One morning, I found a dog hanging around my tent, moaning as only a begging canine can do. She was a tricolor bitch of indeterminate breed: medium-sized, skinny, and short haired. I gave her a couple of the dreaded soya links, and she scarfed them down. When she resumed her earlier vocalizations, I named her Mona. For the rest of the day, she followed me wherever I went. When I fed her again, she adopted me. From that time on, we were inseparable. She would go to the beach with me, and I would go with her on exercise runs—temporarily resuming the Kenyanlike training I had begun years before in school.

The only places to run were on the roads made by our trucks. There weren't many of them, and it was forbidden to leave them for fear of land mines. Mona loved these jaunts, staying close and returning afterward to camp for a reward of soya links. She became the squadron mascot, the soya-link-sausage dog, and I was her official master. She was loved by all and was with us for several months. Then, as mysteriously as she appeared, she was gone. I hoped that she had been adopted by a Bedouin, rather than going off for a run by herself and fatally stepping off the trail.

## Freezing My Gizzard: International Falls—1984

I didn't want to wait for spring to make my effort to prove Jack Moran wrong, so Bob and I signed up for the Freeze Y'r Gizzard Blizzard Run in International Falls, close to the Canadian border. It was the third weekend of January, probably the coldest imaginable time of year. At the race start, it was minus-24 degrees—not conditions under which the average person would attempt to run a personal record.

At the time, I was performing a one-man show called *Expressions of Aging*, whose title I have adopted for this book. Now 60, I knew that many people considered me to be old, but I certainly didn't feel like whatever it is that a person that age is supposed to feel like. The show had been sponsored by the Minnesota Humanities Commission, which had been thrilled to find a professional actor teaching in Bemidji, and the night before the race I scheduled a performance as part of the prerace festivities.

Performing is a lot like running: it requires total concentration and finding what runners call "the zone," where you're so alert and focused that you do what you need to do each moment, without worrying about what comes next. Even the preparation is like warming up for a race. I had done the show many times, but it had a great many lines, and I practiced them in my motel room to make sure that when the time came, I would forget nothing important.

Normally, prerace jitters are one of the toughest parts of racing. But with the need to do the show first, I thought nothing of the race until the day of the big event.

The morning was as cold as advertised, but I remained relaxed about my plans, even as I stripped to a single layer of clothing: tights and a long-sleeve T-shirt (plus, of course, the obligatory plastic bag). My normal four layers of clothing were too heavy and too restrictive, making me feel more like another Minnesota symbol, the Pillsbury Doughboy, than a national-class athlete about to make his mark. But it was difficult to warm up. I loosened up as best I could with a one-mile jog and then retreated to the high-school gym to stretch and keep as warm as possible until the final moments before the start.

The race directors were well aware of our plight. After all, they had been conducting this event for years. They waited until two minutes before the start before summoning us from the gym, then wasted as little time as possible getting us assembled. As we waited, a fog of steam rose from our bodies; then the gun sounded and we were off.

The course was out-and-back, finishing at the school, where the gym would provide warm showers and food. A 40:00 10K is a 6:26 pace, but I wanted to go about six seconds per mile faster in the first miles so I could have a bit of cushion if I slowed later on. I went through the first mile at 6:15—too fast, but not bad—then passed the second at 12:38, almost exactly on target.

One of the advantages of an out-and-back course is that you can see what's happening in the front of the pack as you approach the turnaround. In the lead was my buddy Bob. I waved and shouted, and then I too was at the turnaround, in 19:26—way ahead of goal. Amazingly, I didn't feel the cold.

Mile four was slower but still on pace: a 6:24. All I needed now was to run a pair of 6:45s, kick a bit, and I would have it. Tiring, I concentrated on maintaining an easy, fluid stride and the quick leg turnover recommended by Bob. Mile five went by, and a couple of minutes later, there was Bob, jogging back along the course to pick me up and pace me to the finish. He had won; now it was my turn.

The final 1,200 meters was on packed snow, lumpy in some places and slippery in others. But I had plenty of extra time in the bank, and negotiating this with my training partner beside me, I hit the finish in 39:24. I hadn't just broken my personal record—I had beaten every runner older than 45. I would eventually lower my 10K personal record to 36:32, but that run in the cold and snow remains one of the most satisfying of my life.

And yet, I still had trouble believing I really was all that good. My self-image was improving, but the moment anyone labeled me an athlete, I wanted to deny it. To me, the only people who deserved to be called that in public were professional: superbly fit and generally paid extraordinary amounts of money. I was just a voice teacher from Bemidji, or maybe the boy smothering incendiaries in the London Blitz, so blithely convinced of his own immortality that he didn't see anything unusual in what he was doing. It would take a marathon to make my change in self-image truly stick. And of course, in Minnesota there was only one marathon that mattered.

## CHAPTER 3

# Marathon Roots

*G*reece—1942–44

Africa convinced me that whatever I did after the war would involve nurturing the threads of humanity I had in common with the German artist. The rest of my wartime experiences helped focus that interest on the theater. We remained in North Africa for several more months, advancing from Tobruk to Benghazi and finally to Tripoli, where we met up with the Americans and Rommel was defeated. Then we were posted to Greece to assist mopping-up operations against the remnants of the German occupation force. As wartime assignments go, it was quite pleasant because we were among a populace that was delighted to receive us, and there was plenty of time to sample the local culture.

To many young soldiers, "culture" might be limited to taverns, but for me, somewhat to my surprise, it included trips to as many historic sites as I could find time to visit.

Greece reawakened my childhood interest in the theater. My favorite places were the ancient, open-air amphitheaters. There, I would climb onto marble stages that once heard ancient Greek plays and strut back and forth, mumbling poems remembered from school and pretending I was a great actor, holding an audience in the palm of his hand. Sometimes, I was tempted to recite full voice, but Greek officials and other servicemen were always nearby, and I was too shy.

I was now 19 and fascinated with all things Greek. I decided to learn the language, picking it up so easily that it was almost as though I already knew it and merely needed to brush up. My squadron mates were stunned. Each day, I collected a few new words. Each evening, I practiced making up sentences with them, carrying out make-believe conversations while settling down to bed. The next day, I would practice all of the new words while learning others. It was yet another skill I would need in theater: the ability to learn vast amounts of dialogue, quickly and surely.

Greece was also where I laid the first true foundations for my future singing career. I had always loved to sing and had done so at every opportunity, but now I practiced my Greek by learning love songs. They were fun and made me popular in a village a couple of miles from our camp, where my friends and I would often visit. We could get meals there, cheap and delicious, as welcome as the Bedouin eggs had been in North Africa. Even the bars, with their ouzo and retsina, always served hors d'oeuvres.

In part, our welcome was due to the fact that the Germans had been brutal occupiers. But my growing facility with the language made me doubly welcome.

One bar owner asked me to sing for the residents of a hospital for the disabled. I was flattered and told him so. Many of the residents had been hurt in the resistance. Simply knowing that they who had suffered the worst the Nazis could dish out wanted to hear me sing was an incredible honor—not to mention the sweet music of applause that rewarded me afterward.

The visit was repeated, then became a regular event on which I was usually accompanied by one or two friends. In addition to the music, our uniformed presence was a recurring confirmation that the Germans were gone. Through these patients, we had the opportunity to share the joy of an entire nation.

One small ward accommodated only four patients, all girls who had received spinal injuries that rendered them paraplegic. One was about my age: a stunning beauty with dark, sparkling eyes, jet-black hair, and a radiantly pale complexion. Her name was Kiki, and her affliction had nothing to do with the Nazis; she had fallen from a horse on rough terrain. She had a devastatingly infectious smile, and my friends and I never failed to find ourselves sharing her continuing joy and enthusiasm for life.

The medical staff told me her condition was irreversible. But she thought otherwise, and many times I would sit with her, holding her hand and listening to her plan her future. Of the songs I sang, she particularly loved one called "Thio Mavra Matia," which told of a man's love for a dark-eyed beauty. When I sang, her gaze produced such a lump in my throat that sometimes I could hardly finish.

Kiki and her roommates urged me to come daily, and I did my best to do so, even though I knew she yearned for the impossible day when she would leave her bed and we would be married. Meanwhile, I cherished her sweet, radiant spirit—and, at 19, learned much from her about courage, loving, and life. Then our squadron was posted to a new assignment. We held each other and cried, and then I had to leave because such are the ways of war.

## The Wrong Person's Advice: Twin Cities Marathon— 1985

I would be well into my sixties before I could finally accept the title of "athlete" without flinching. But secretly I had always relished the privilege of winning. And I liked the fact that I always finished in the top 10 percent of racers of all ages. In 1985, I contacted the Twin Cities Marathon again, and this time I had the right stuff to show race director Jack Moran. My 39:24 10K, especially run under less than ideal conditions, spoke for itself. I might still have lingering self-doubts, but the 10K clearly said I could go up against Alex Ratelle.

And so it was that at dawn on a chilly October morning, I found myself beneath the "P" of the Pillsbury Building—one of the race's sponsors—waiting for the starting gun that would set off my first marathon. Behind me, many runners had punched arm- and head-holes into garbage bags and were wearing them as throwaway warm-ups to be discarded a mile or so into the race, but in my part of the pack, everyone was stripped to T-shirts and shorts. We have a term for that in the far north: "Minnesota macho"—the desire never to give an inch to the weather, no matter what it is. And, as at the Freeze Y'r Gizzard Blizzard Run, I knew I would be comfortable once I got started, so I didn't want to waste even one precious second dealing with a garbage bag or other warm-up a few meters into the race.

I was running well in the first miles when I got to talking to a younger man and told him it was my first marathon. He looked at me sharply and offered a bit of well-intentioned advice: "You're going a bit fast for a first attempt." Just as I had heeded Bob's suggestion when he told me to shorten my stride,

I immediately did as this fellow recommended. It was only much later that I realized that in doing so in the middle of a race for which I had prepared for so long, I was actually listening to my own self-doubts. Bob's advice had felt right the moment I heard it, and I had verified it by repeated testing. This advice I listened to simply because I didn't trust myself.

Ratelle was somewhere ahead, heeding his own advice. Because I heeded someone else's, I ran a 3:23. But it was by no means a disaster because all the way, I felt strong and comfortable.

At mile 20, someone had constructed a massive theatrical set of a stone wall with an archway through which the runners passed. It was intended to commemorate the mark at which many runners, hitting the infamous "wall," begin to falter, but for me, it was an intriguing juxtaposition of my youthful chase after theatrical success with my new career as a racing star in the making. Just as then I had passed through many obstacles en route to eventual success, now I passed through the faux wall without ever hitting the real one. At the finish, I had mixed feelings. I knew I could have run a lot faster. But I was exhilarated because I had finished feeling as though I could run the entire race all over again. Technically, I had even beaten Alex, because he had pulled out somewhere late in the race, but beating him that way didn't count.

Next time, I would give him a run for his money. Next time, I would be a *lot* faster.


## AWOL in Athens: Greece—1944

Greece had been more than merely another stop along the Mediterranean. It felt like a new home, and I did not want to leave. During the Blitz, I had felt the camaraderie that had united me with all the people of London. Here, I felt even greater camaraderie. Everyone had a common goal: the elimination of tyranny and the return to a calmer, more caring way of life. I was tired of the war and longed to share that goal with them.

Our squadron was being moved to Italy. In the truck carrying us to the boat, I decided I wanted to become a true Greek. When the truck slowed at a corner, I jumped out the back and ran. Then I started walking, heading for the downtown of what had become my beloved Athens. What I was doing was almost unimaginable. I was a deserter, and if I was caught, I would be in enormous trouble. It was one of the most unutterably stupid things I have ever done.

As I made my way toward the center of town, I met a Greek sailor. We chatted a while—in Greek—and then he asked me where I was going. I told him I didn't know; I had just deserted the RAF. That puzzled him, and he asked why I had been in the RAF. Had I been living in England when the war broke out? Had I been there to learn English? His questions made me realize that my Greek was now so good I could actually pass for Greek. Even at the time, I found it amazing but felt compelled to admit I was indeed English.

He was a little drunk and in the mood to become more so, so he invited me to a tavern where, over a couple of glasses of ouzo, he suggested that since I loved his country so much, I should indeed stay. His mother and father could shelter me, he boozily informed me, until the RAF wrote me off as dead or missing in action.

In the camaraderie of ouzo, I was sorely tempted to accept his offer. It was obvious that I should be his brother. But as we left the bar, two British military police officers drove by in a jeep. I was still wearing my uniform, but a serviceman and a Greek enjoying the town together didn't raise eyebrows. They were passing by without incident when, as quickly as it had hit, the desire to desert vanished. From one heartbeat to the next, I realized the foolishness of what I was doing and wanted to be back with my squadron. Quickly begging leave of my new friend, I ran for the jeep and flagged it down.

The MPs took me to their commander, who straightaway took me back to my squadron. There, I was again marched into the CO's office, but this time, there was no way he would commend me for patriotism. Cap respectfully removed, I listened to him inform me that I was under house arrest. Then, because my service record was to this point unblemished and because I had turned myself in, he told me that my sentence would be lenient and I would have to serve only two weeks confined to barracks once we reached Italy.

What I did not know was that once I got out of the barracks, Italy would affect me even more deeply and lastingly than Greece had.

# CHAPTER 4

# Getting Serious

*G*randma's Marathon: Duluth, Minnesota—1986

Perhaps my early love of Greece planted the seeds that would later mature into my love of the marathon. Perhaps I would have discovered the marathon anyway. Who can tell? The ways of the soul are mysterious indeed.

As any distance runner knows, the marathon dates from 490 BC, when a message bearer named Pheidippides was dispatched from Marathon to Athens with news of a critical victory. According to legend, he staggered to the city center, croaked "Nike" (the goddess of victory, from whom the shoe company took its name), and promptly collapsed and died. It's a great story, though there is some doubt about its accuracy. Pheidippides was a real person, but he was a trained military message runner who appears to have twice covered 140 miles in 36 hours. If a mere 26.2 miles did him in, it must have been a fluke.

The now-standard marathon distance wasn't established until 1904. In the first modern Olympics, held in Athens in 1896, the distance was about 24 miles. Four years later, in St. Louis, it had increased to 25, but in the sporting world, "marathon" merely meant "long road race," and nobody cared about precision.

In 1904, the Olympics were scheduled for London and the distance was increased again, to 26 miles. But officials wanted the finish to be opposite Queen Victoria's box in White City stadium, so the race was extended an extra 385 yards. Since then, all marathons have been precisely 26 miles, 385 yards (which, incidentally, is about 30 yards longer than 26.2 miles).

My second attempt at the distance came in June of my 61st year, at Grandma's Marathon in Duluth. It and Twin Cities are Minnesota's premier distance-running events, and Grandma's—the older race—has a storied history highlighted by some exceedingly fast finishes. This time, I wasn't heeding anybody's advice but my own. I ran my race, at my pace, and finished in 2:58:23, more than 24 minutes faster than I had run Twin Cities. This time, Alex didn't drop out of the race, and I finished behind him to take second in our age group.

•  •  •

I now believe that runners who take up running later in life need about seven or eight years to reach their peak performances. During that time, they are building a training base and gaining experience. Once they reach that peak, they can sustain it for maybe three or four years before the continuing advance of years offsets whatever additional gains there might be from training and experience.

I had been racing for five years. I did not yet know where my apex might lie, but I knew I had yet to reach it. There was no reason I couldn't continue improving well into my sixties.

## Italy—1944–46

Greece was where I made my first serious efforts at singing, but Italy was where I took my first steps toward making it a career. First, though, I had to wait for the war to end. I served my confinement peeling potatoes (really!) and then was transferred to a base near Naples and from there to Rome. Thankfully, I was no longer anywhere close to the fighting and served the next few months preparing aircraft to be returned to England for use in the invasion of Normandy. We were also preparing a fleet of troop-carrying gliders for a supposed parachute and glider invasion of southern Germany, to be launched across the Alps from Italy. But the Germans were in full retreat and the war was over before the gliders were ready.

There being a sudden decline in the need for airplane mechanics, I was transferred back to Naples as an accountant in the RAF's administrative offices. Accounting and I weren't the best fit, and the only useful skill I retained from that era was the ability to organize data. Most runners are sloppy about maintaining running logs—a shame because it's extremely useful to be able to look back at how you trained in prior years and see how it affected your results. Thanks to the RAF, my running logs are unusually precise and comprehensive. At the time, though, accounting seemed pretty dull.

Still, there were benefits to being in a large city, one of which was access to professional-grade entertainment. The U.S. forces fared particularly well on that score, thanks to the ministrations of the USO, and we British were always welcome guests. I particularly remember a concert in which the Andrews Sisters were paired with Glenn Miller. It renewed my love of music, and I resolved to continue to work on my own singing. How I would do so, though, I had no idea.

Sometimes, a friend named Ray and I would head into Naples to eat, drink, and cruise for girls. The first two pursuits were always successful, the latter usually not. Young Italian women were generally accompanied by chaperones who did not approve of soldiers out on the town. But a few balked at tradition. One time, two of them urged Ray and me to take them to the opera.

I had never been to an opera before, but the girl was another dark-eyed beauty, and anyway, I loved music of all kinds. I remember everything about the opera. It was at the San Carlo Opera House, which would figure prominently in a later episode of my life, and I was particularly impressed with the tenor who sang the "Flower Song" from *Carmen*. Eighteen years later, I would perform the same role myself in one of the greatest university music departments in North America.

• • •

As Ray and I continued our forays, I was learning Italian with the same felicity I had previously had for Greek. It certainly didn't hurt us in the hunt for dates, allowing me to combine the appeal of a foreigner with the ability to converse like a native. On another outing, we met another pair of women, Mariolina and Pupa, on the Via Caracciolo, the main seaside promenade through Naples. Ray paired off with Pupa, but I was immediately smitten with Mariolina, who was a five-foot-five northern-Italian beauty with movie-star looks, blonde hair, and blue eyes. She was on an extended visit from her home near Torino—another place that would later feature prominently in my future. Mariolina shared my nascent love of opera, and we went to hear it, time and again.

• • •

One of the oddities of war is that when it is over, life accelerates, as though trying to make up for lost time. In America, half a generation of young men crammed through college in three years on the GI bill, forgoing summer breaks in a rush to get back the years lost to the war.

I got married.

It was 1946, I was 21, had known Mariolina only a few months, and we were in love. We both enjoyed music, opera, and theater. The difference was that she loved attending them, while I was already plotting ways of being in them. That's an enormous difference, because I had even more dues to pay in becoming an actor than I would later pay in becoming a runner.

## Upstaged in L.A.: North American Road Races—1985–1993

When I took up running, I had been in living in Bemidji for six years. By the time I took second place at Grandma's, it had risen to 10 years, the longest I had spent in any location other than my boyhood home.

I don't know whether I realized it when I married Mariolina, but acting is a transient's profession. Although there would always be a home base, it would be hard for me to count the number of boarding houses, motels, and, as success came my way, luxury hotels in which I made extended stays.

Now I was ready to take my running show on the road, as well. The advantage was that each performance is by necessity a one-time stand. Even an encore has to wait for next year's race.

My training logs tell the story. In the early 1980s, I ran local races, mostly in Minnesota. In 1986, I was beginning to travel, doing 20 races in six states. In 1987, an injury truncated my season in April, but in 1988, I was back in form. This was also the era in which I set my lifetime personal bests. In 1990, I ran 37:42 for 10K (a year later, I bettered that time by more than a minute, but it was on a downhill course), and in the same year I ran 29:29 for the 8K and 17:47 for the 5K. A year later, at age 66, I ran 58:50 for the 15K. I didn't run many half-marathons, but my PR, also set in 1991, was 1:23:16.

But the marathon continued to be my premier event. By the time I was 65, I had run four more of them below the three-hour mark. The first was on a return trip to the Twin Cities Marathon, in 1986, when I ran 2:55:53 and took first in my age division (Alex Ratelle wasn't there). My best came in the 1987 Los Angeles Marathon, where I ran 2:52:38—a 6:36 pace. I assumed I had won my age division again because Alex hadn't been there, but even though I asked several officials, nobody could tell me, one way or the other. After an hour with no definitive answer, I gave up because I had a plane to catch right after the race. I had scheduled it so soon because, while I had enjoyed the marathon, I had hated Los Angeles. After living among the trees and lakes of northern Minnesota, I found L.A.'s sprawling, polluted mess an intolerable shock. There are cities that I like—San Francisco, Portland, and Naples are three—but Los Angeles will never be among them.

I was on a brief West Coast sabbatical and wouldn't be heading straight home, so I called home and asked my family to track down the results. It took a day or two, but eventually they discovered that Dick Van Dyke (he of *Mary Poppins* fame!) had crossed the line ahead of me. I didn't know Dick Van Dyke personally, but in his television and movie roles, he certainly looked like a runner. But to have pulled a world-class time out of thin air? How could he have managed it?

I stewed about that for several days. *Good for him*, I thought, practicing the line to myself. But I couldn't hide my disappointment.

Finally, I told a friend, who found the story as dubious as I did. He immediately called the marathon office. "Oh, no," someone told him. "Dick Van Dyke was part of a relay team from Hollywood. There were 26 of them and they each ran a mile." In fact, the race officials told my friend, I had not only won my age group, I had been 243rd out of 15,000 starters.

I had run the race of my life and scored a personal record. But for four days, I had been feeling upstaged by another actor-turned-runner. Now I learned that I had been beaten by a relay team—not so bad after all.

# Demobbed and Unemployed: Italy–London–Italy—1946–47

I was officially demobilized from the RAF—"demobbed" we called it—sometime in 1946. As a result, Mariolina and I found ourselves in London, without a very clear plan.

The adventurous teenager who had left five years before was now a 21-year-old man with a wife—and a baby on the way. What I *needed* was money. What I *wanted* was to continue my education in music. The ideal solution would be a scholarship similar to the one I had been offered in art, all those years before. I auditioned for London's Trinity School of Music and was accepted. As a veteran, I was entitled to certain benefits, including educational grants, so I did the obvious and applied for a scholarship. But the government wasn't in the mood to fund the arts. What it wanted were bricklayers, carpenters, and electricians for the rebuilding of London. Scholarship money in those fields was abundant, but if I took it, I would never find my way back to the career I wanted. Frustrated, Mariolina, our new baby, and I headed back for a land where we had a place to stay and where I might be able to do everything.

In Italy, I had one truly marketable skill that had the added advantage of not requiring me to risk more hernias by lifting heavy objects: by now I could speak Italian like a native. So, Mariolina, baby Anthony, and I moved in with her sister in Naples, and I took a job as an interpreter for a man who bought U.S. Army surplus equipment for resale in Italy. The job was perfect because it paid enough that I could afford voice lessons. All I needed was a good teacher.

I found him via the San Carlo Opera House, where I had seen my first opera two years before. I had been making inquiries all over town, but it was at the stage door of the San Carlo that someone informed me that the best voice teacher in Naples was Professor Alfredo Morelli.

My memory of our first meeting is as vivid today as it was then. Morelli was a plump, benign-looking 70-year-old, whose studio was a large living room in his surprisingly ordinary third-floor apartment. It was a dark room, its walls covered with pictures of past opera stars. Throw rugs draped an overstuffed sofa and a large easy chair sat beside a small table on which sheets of music lay scattered. The professor was sipping from an espresso cup as his wife led me to the door, and he continued to sip as he waved me to an armchair. It was an old chair, low to the ground, and as I lowered myself into it, it enveloped me in a way that made me feel diminutive in this great man's presence.

On the far side of the room, a large upright piano stood close to a set of French windows, whose reflected daylight glinted from the piano's music holder. I was extremely nervous and became even more so when introduced to the professor's wife, a former opera diva whose name I recognized, even though she was now well into her sixties.

Before my visit, I had learned enough about the professor's history to be very intimidated. Formerly a famous musical director and opera conductor, he was now president of one of Italy's best music schools, the Conservatorio di San Pietro a Majella, in Naples. Here in his home, he taught a select group of private students.

His wife, the former diva, offered me tea. As she served it, I explained that I was working as a translator but was in Italy primarily so I could learn to sing professionally. I told them that it was impossible to do this in England because the country wanted carpenters, not musicians.

The professor shook his head at the world's sad ways. *Allora facciamo l'audizione*, he said. "Let us audition. What have you brought?"

"Nothing, I'm afraid."

"Do you know 'Che Gelida Manina' from *La Boheme*?"

I said that I was familiar with that aria but that it ended with a high C that I would be unable to hit.

"Do not be concerned about that," the professor said. "At this stage, that is not important." Then he began the piano introduction.

Doing an important audition without choking on nerves is like reaching the starting line of a race both energized and relaxed. It takes years of practice, and some people never really master it. Knowing that this was the most important musical performance of my life made me far too nervous, and having to negotiate the high note at the end by singing it falsetto did nothing to improve my confidence.

When I finished, the professor looked at me and then back to the music. Then he looked at me again, and again he waved me toward the all-enveloping armchair. Never taking his eyes off me, he rose from the piano, moved to his own chair, and lowered his aging frame into it. Clearly, the news would not be good.

"I'm sorry. I'm afraid you just don't have that good a voice. I cannot in good conscience take your money."

In a flash I was taken back to elementary school, being told by the music teacher that I couldn't be in the choir because I couldn't sing.

Then, seeing that I was nearly in tears, the professor preempted my next question with a gentle offer. "Perhaps," he said, "we could try ten lessons. If during that time, you make sufficient progress, we can continue your studies. If not, the ten are free."

• • •

My first lesson was two days later. I was still feeling diminutive but I had nine more opportunities to prove myself, and the immediate pressure was abated. Ten minutes into the lesson, when we had done nothing more than a few vocal exercises, my teacher again looked up from the music. "I'm sorry," he said. "I was badly mistaken. You have a very pretty tenor voice."

And so it was that I began my training with this fine old man and his wife, who came to treat me as though I were their own son. Often, the professor would call his wife in so she could hear me sing a phrase or two or sometimes a whole aria, after which he would brag to her yet again about his new English tenor.

I was taking lessons daily now, which taxed my financial resources to the limit. Normally I would take the streetcar to the professor's home. But I had not yet managed to kick a cigarette habit that I had picked up during the war, and often there wasn't money for both the streetcar and cigarettes—even though I smoked one or two a day and could buy them individually from kids on the street.

On those days, I would use my streetcar fare to buy a cigarette and then run the two miles from my lodgings to the professor's. There, not having touched the cigarette because I wanted my voice to be at its best, I would sing my lesson, then relax by smoking half of it afterward. Then I would extinguish it, put the other half in my pocket, and run home, saving the remainder for another day. Smoking isn't recommended either for runners or singers, but being so poor that you can afford only half a cigarette—and then only by running four miles for it—is probably a good formula for keeping the habit from doing you serious damage.

## California International Marathon: Sacramento— 1988

I was one day shy of my 64th birthday when I finally beat Alex Ratelle. The race was the California International Marathon, which is held on a lightning-fast course in Sacramento. At least, it's fast as long as the weather's good. It's a long, gentle downgrade, with just enough small bounces to keep it interesting, running from the northeastern suburbs to the state capitol. Normally, December weather in Sacramento resembles early October in Minnesota, with golden leaves catching morning sun and just enough chill in the air to keep you cool. But there have been years when the race is run into the teeth of an early-winter storm fresh off the Pacific. Then, it's into the wind the whole way, and the Californians, at least, think it's cold.

That year, 1988, was one of the good years. The day was fresh and crisp, and I was eager to go. I knew that Alex was there, and this time, I was going to get him.

At the gun, he took off ahead of me, and I let him go. In Olympic marathons, the leaders often stay bunched so that they can have company and keep track of each other, but among the age-group elite, there is no such need. You are running largely against the clock, and there are always plenty of younger runners for company. Besides, you get your best results by running your own race, and Alex's early pace was too hot for my taste.

He was never far ahead, though, and somewhere around mile seven, I reeled him in. We had been racing against each other now for three years, and as fellow Minnesotans we had seen a lot of each other and become friends. So, while having me go by him so early in the race probably wasn't something he had hoped to see, his reaction was to call encouragement. "Looking good, John," he said. "There's another guy in our age group just ahead. Go get him!"

There is only one proper reaction to advice like that, and that is to chase the other runner. I went after him and eventually got him. Alex dropped out. It was the fourth-fastest marathon of my life, with a time of 2:54:36. It was also the last time Alex severely challenged me. He had been at the top of his game for years, whereas I was fresh and new. By the time I turned 65, the upper-sixties age group was mine to win.

## Gigli's Doorstep: Naples–Rome–London—1947

My singing was becoming good enough that my professor was comparing me to one of his former pupils, Mirto Picchi, now a tenor in high demand in opera houses throughout Italy. Other than a continued deficit of money, my musical future looked brighter and brighter, and I was beginning to learn a small repertoire of songs, mostly less demanding than "Che Gelida Manina," ranging from other arias to "Danny Boy."

Then, after six months of daily lessons, it all came crashing down. I was in my employer's apartment/office, discussing his next purchase of army trucks or electrical generators, when there was a knock at the door. His wife opened it, and three uniformed *carabinieri* marched in, saying they had to make a search. Within minutes they found what they had come for: three thousand black-market American dollars, which my employer had been obtaining with illicit sales of some of his military-surplus property. I was in no way implicated, but my employer's business was over and so, in a flash, was my job.

I struggled through two more weeks of lessons, many of them free. But paying for lessons wasn't the worst of my concerns. Without a job, I could no longer feed my family.

The only option was to go back to London while I could still afford to, find some kind of work there, and carry on as best I could.

The Chunnel (the tunnel beneath the English Channel) hadn't yet been built, but the cheapest way back to England was nevertheless by rail, plus ferry. The first leg of our journey was to Rome, where we were scheduled to change trains. But carrying my luggage through the station, I was struck by a fierce, stabbing pain in my groin. It was yet another hernia, far more sudden and excruciating than anything I had experienced before.

The stationmaster saw me collapse and rushed me to his personal physician. That doctor took one look at me and said I had a strangulated hernia—a condition in which a loop of the intestine pokes through the lower abdominal wall and is choked off by the pressure. By that time, the word "strangulated" sounded about right. My entire torso was rigid from the pain, and I was feeling a choking sensation as far up as my neck. Lower down, the pain focused in a hard, rocklike lump that projected on the right side of my abdomen.

The doctor told me I needed immediate medical attention—something I had, by now, already deduced—and proceeded to deliver it on the spot. Pressing on the lump and rotating it with a massagelike motion, he forced it back through the rupture in the abdominal wall, sliding it back into place with a distinct clicking sensation.

Instantly, the tightness released. Only then did the doctor explain the peril that I had been in. The protruding loop of intestine had been so tightly constricted that it was receiving no blood flow. Without treatment, it would have died within hours, requiring major surgery to remove the dead tissue before it turned gangrenous. Somewhat amazingly, the doctor also told me that I could continue to London, although I would be advised to avail myself of the services of a porter. There was only one problem: we had missed our train.

During my examination and treatment, Mariolina and baby Tony had been waiting with the stationmaster in the doctor's anteroom. Mariolina had told him about my voice lessons and the reason we were returning to London, and now the stationmaster took charge of the situation. His name was Caligaris. A kindly man close to retirement age, he informed me in limited English that the three of us would be spending the night with him. I wasn't in a position to argue, and he wouldn't have relented had I tried.

That night, over dinner, I learned that he and his wife were opera lovers and that he had seen every opera in the Italian repertoire. Why in heaven's name, he asked, did the young English singer want to go back to England when he could stay here and continue his education?

Running a big-city train station was an important job, and he was an influential man in Rome, well connected in operatic circles. He could arrange for me to meet the great Italian tenor Beniamino Gigli for voice lessons. He knew he could make this happen because he had accommodated Gigli's travel arrangements on numerous occasions, and the tenor was his personal friend.

Gigli was world renowned. No less than Caruso's successor to the accolade of "greatest tenor in the world," he was now into his sixth decade but still a vital man whose voice showed no aging, although he now spent as much time teaching as performing.

Caligaris couldn't have come up with a more tempting offer. During my prior return to England, I had acquired several of Gigli's records and had listened over and over, trying to emulate his sound. He was my singing idol, and I longed to be able to produce such brilliantly resonant tones.

Shortly before I had to leave Naples, Professor Morelli had told me that I no longer sounded like Mirto Picchi. Instead, I was beginning to develop a vocal tone similar to Beniamino Gigli. And now, I had a chance not only to meet my hero but to be tutored by him.

Caligaris was as good as his word, but again, there was only one problem: Gigli was away and not expected back for two months. We learned this from his housekeeper, standing on the steps of his spacious villa. How on earth was I to keep myself and my family fed, clothed, and housed for two months?

Caligaris pulled every string he could think of to find a way to get me sponsored until Gigli's return. He even offered to put us up in his own apartment for however long it took for me to become financially solvent. But two weeks of that was all that I could accept. Besides, we were already expecting our second child, Michael, who would be born in London in 1947. My Italian sojourn had at long last come to an end.

## CHAPTER 5

# The Quest

## *O*ldest, But Not Quite Old Enough: Clackamas River Canyon Marathon, Oregon—1994

In May 1994, I ran a marathon in a time of 2:58:33. I was pleased, but it was just one of many good races that year. Months later, Joe Henderson contacted me. An author and frequent contributor to *Runner's World*, Joe loved to prowl though running records, and he had discovered that my performance, just a few days shy of age 69 1/2, made me the oldest person ever to break three hours in a marathon.

Now, I wondered whether I could do it again at 70. A few years before, an organization called the World Association of Veteran Athletes (WAVA) had created a set of age-graded performance tables that let runners compare performances across the years. For each distance and each age up to 99, these charts contain decimal factors showing the amount by which WAVA's experts believed the human body slows down (assuming you've not quit training) compared to what it could have done last year, or last decade, or all the way back to when you were in your twenties or thirties.

According to these charts, a male runner of my age loses about 1 percent of his speed per year—a bit less than two minutes for a three-hour marathoner.

Luckily, I didn't need to wait a full year; I needed to wait only six months. Then, in theory, I would be no more than a minute slower—just enough to have a good chance at squeaking under the three-hour barrier. Even if I couldn't break three hours, I had a good shot at the 70–74 age-group record of 3:01:14, set a few years earlier by Chicagoan Warren Utes—a man whose name had also dotted the record books for my current 65–69 division.

Most people dread those decadal birthdays. How many women are "29 and holding" or "39 and holding?" How many men talk despairingly of "hitting the big three-oh" . . . or "four-oh," "five-oh," "six-oh," etc. An entire cottage industry of birthday cards is designed to rub people's noses in this.

Runners look at it differently: every five years represents a new age group. For young runners, getting older isn't "bad" because of the age, per se, it's because, at least in road races, the competition gets steadily worse. Age-group 25–29 is tougher than 20–24; 30–34 is tougher yet, and most folks complain that nobody but themselves seems to be slowing down at 35–39 or 40–44 (I can't say; I wasn't running at those ages!).

This sense that age does not bring much of a slowdown helps keep young runners from regretting the advance of the years. They're not getting older; they're getting faster. Then come the upper-masters age groups, and now each new division is cause for celebration. If you're competitive, 60 is far better than 59 because now you can beat up on the 64-year-olds, rather than getting beaten up on by the 50-year-olds. In my case, at 70, I had a whole new set of targets to shoot for, and I could hardly wait to take aim at the biggest of all, the marathon.

From 65 to 69, I had been the best in the United States in my age group. Now, I was on a new mission. It would prove to be the toughest I had ever tackled in either my running or my theatrical careers.

## Not Enough Business in Show Business: London— 1947–54

Out-of-work performers are described as "resting." By that standard, the next few years were the best-rested of my life. Though actually, they were rather hectic, as I tried to make the leap from being an aspiring performer to the real thing.

There was no hope in opera. There were only four opera companies in all of the UK, and being told by your voice teacher that you sound like a young Gigli and actually winning a role are very different matters. Besides, my formal training, while intense, was brief by operatic standards, where tenors can prepare for years before actually hitting the stage. I would eventually get my shot at opera, but for the moment, what London offered was theater. For a singer, there were two basic types: musical plays and revues. The difference is that revues are comprised of music, dance, and comedy sketches united by a common theme but with nothing resembling a plot. I would later come to prefer musical plays because (if you picked carefully) they could have fairly long runs and tended to tour less, allowing me to spend more time at home. But beginners can't be choosy.

My voice was more than adequately suited for the chorus in most musicals, but my first audition was painfully reminiscent of my childhood tryout for the school choir. I had followed a casting call to the Hippodrome Theatre in London's West End, where I joined hundreds of others seeking a depressingly small number of jobs. As is common with such auditions, they began with a one-song screening. If you survived that, you advanced to a more thorough audition.

When my turn came, I walked sheepishly onto the stage, head angled low, barely managing to mumble my name when asked. I had been required to bring my own music, and rather than learning an appropriate show tune, I brought something I had studied with Professor Morelli: Schubert's "Serenade." But I had learned it in Italian, and figuring they would rather hear it in their own language, I was planning to do an English version I barely knew. With the pianist sight reading, I launched into the unfamiliar words . . . and was barely started when I heard, "Thank you, Mr. Caston," and that was the end of that.

As I shuffled out onto the street, I couldn't decide which was worse; the way I had ruined my own chances at the part, or being so summarily discharged. But I had one enormous advantage over the little boy who had not sung publicly again for years. Professor Morelli, Caligaris, my parents—all of them believed in me. All said my voice was something special. I have probably always been stubborn, but now my stubbornness had a new focus: I would prove I could do this, no matter how long it took.

• • •

I also learned that it paid to bring the right audition materials and that no matter how much of an impostor you might feel, you really had to be at least reasonably sharp from the first few bars or you were doomed.

After a few more failures, I landed my first part.

It was in the chorus of a musical whose name I have forgotten. After initial rehearsals, we toured the provinces, working out the kinks, then came home for our London opener. My parents were thrilled, but the show lasted only three weeks more, and then I was resting again. But at least I now had an actual stage credit and wasn't merely another "wannabe." In the next seven years, that would lead to a half-dozen more musicals and three or four revues.

"Resting," though, continued to be a major occupation. And the roles I did get typically paid poorly enough that, during the interludes, day jobs were critical. Sometimes, I even had to keep the day job while performing. That was easy when the show was in London and not impossible if I was on the road. In one traveling revue, I had a job selling furniture polish. By day, I would ply my wares door-to-door; at night, I would sing—baritone, in this instance. Partway through the run, a newspaper learned of this and did a feature about me, calling me the baritone with polish. Someday, I thought, maybe I would get a role large enough to draw a similar review of my abilities at something more than door knocking.

• • •

My training was in music, but the primary component of any play, even a musical, is acting. Even being in the chorus is an acting job because you're part of all the crowd scenes. Occasionally, though, I landed small supporting roles instead, the type of thing that gets you one good song and a few lines of dialogue. I worked hard at these, knowing my future depended on both skills.

The need for work meant I occasionally took parts in slipshod productions or worked for tightwad producers no established performer would work with. Once, I even took a role under an assumed name. It was a traveling production where nobody was going to recognize me, and while it paid a pittance, there was enough to send some home to Mariolina. And so it continued for several years, as I learned my craft and waited for my big break.

## Seventy at Last: McMinnville, Oregon— December 5, 1994

My 70th birthday found me in Oregon, where I had moved after retiring from teaching in 1991. December isn't as cold there as in Minnesota, but it's a damp cold that can be more miserable than Bemidji's sunnier, icicle-in-your-scarf days. There is a limit to how many miles you want to run in the rain, and most Pacific Northwest runners cut back in the winter. But I had no intention of wasting time. I had been on one of the greatest racing streaks of my life. The week before my 2:58 marathon, I had run the second-fastest

15K of my life, covering the 9.3 miles in 58:02—a pace of 6:14 per mile. The week afterward, I had bounced back well enough to run a 5K in 18:55, a 6:06 pace.

I doubt that a coach in the country would recommend such a schedule. Most racing gurus advise a full day's recovery for each mile raced, which would have meant nine days for the 15K and nearly a month between the marathon and the 5K. Additional time is needed to prep for each race, and to "taper" from intense training so you will be ready and rested.

Somehow, I didn't seem to think these rules applied to me. Before turning 70, I picked up four single-age world track records for 69-year-olds: 10,000 meters in 38:30; 5,000 meters in 18:36; 3,000 meters in 10:54, and the mile at 5:34.8.

A few days after my 70th birthday, I ran a world's-best half-marathon for the 70–74 age group, in 1:25:04 (a 6:29 pace). A world's best is a time that would have been a world record had it been done on a certified racecourse, and if the course was measured by people generally known for getting it right, the mark still carries considerable weight. I was strong, fit, and confident of achieving my marathon goal.

I had chosen to make the attempt at the Houston Marathon, in mid-January. In the three weeks immediately preceding my half-marathon, I had logged 49 miles, 62 miles, and 48 miles. In the four weeks between it and the marathon, I cut my weekly mileage to 35, logging only 17 in the five days before the race. I might have raced too often the year before, but for once, I was not only in perfect racing shape but also well tuned and rested. It would be the last time in a long time I would enter a race so well prepared.

•  •  •

I hadn't just registered for the marathon. I had told the race directors what I was planning, and they had issued a formal invitation, treating me much as they treated the young elites seeking the top prizes. The race was on Sunday, so I arrived well in advance, on Wednesday evening. The next morning, with the other elites, I attended a press conference and then went sightseeing. That afternoon, I remembered that in Las Vegas, prior to getting my world's-best half-marathon, my final hard training session had consisted of running several times from the first floor to the 25th floor of the Stardust Hotel. Like many actors, I can be superstitious, so now I spent 35 minutes doing the same in my hotel in Houston. Then, along with the other elite runners, I went to dinner at a Greek Orthodox church.

The dinner was a major event because the Houston Marathon has a special relationship with a marathon in Athens. Each year, the fastest Houstonites, male and female, got a free trip to Greece, and the fastest Athenians came to Houston. The dinner was to honor the Greek participants, with whom I had a chance to practice my somewhat rusty Greek.

The meal, a buffet, featured moussaka served from large flat pans. The volunteer servers gave me the last piece from one pan, while the folks behind me got moussaka from a fresh pan, just out of the oven.

That night, I awoke at 3:00 A.M. with horrible cramps that kept me running to the bathroom with a lot more urgency than I had felt previously, running stairs. In the morning, I learned that half of the other elite runners were in the same state. With one piece of moussaka from the wrong tray, we had gone from superbly fit to unable to stray more than a few paces from the nearest toilet. My mood was bleak, but determined. I had 48 hours to shake the bug and recover my fitness. If it could be done, I would do it.

## Covent Garden, London—Circa 1952

Theater work was erratic (and paltry), and my family was continuing to grow. Michael was born in 1947. He was followed three years later by Philip. Much as I wanted to devote myself solely to the stage, the day jobs kept the boys clothed, housed, and fed.

I also received assistance from a military pension, which paid me the not-so-princely sum of seven shillings a week because I was considered partially disabled by my hernias. After that initial surgery in Alexandria, there had been six other operations in Africa, Greece, and Italy. Now I was called back for one "final" repair that would fix it once and for all. "You're going to be all right this time," the surgeon told me afterward. "We put some concrete in there." Actually, what he had used was wire mesh, and the result was too good, because it impeded blood flow and required yet another surgery a year or two later to deal with that. Thanks to the hernia and related procedures, I spent far too much of my younger years in hospitals. The bright side is that by comparison, running injuries are usually trivial, and the hernia experiences taught me more than I wanted to know about how to be patient while they healed.

Meanwhile, I was considered cured, so the military took away my pension. That made the day jobs more important than ever, and I had to look for positions that paid better than door-to-door sales.

One was as "empties manager" for a wholesale produce company in Covent Garden, the largest fruit and vegetable market in England. Farmers from as far as one hundred miles away would bring in their produce during the night for sale to wholesalers, who then distributed it throughout the city. The result was a madhouse from midnight until noon the following day.

My job was to keep track of the empty produce crates returned by the retailers—not all that different from some of the accounting work I did during my last months with the RAF. I would come to work about 5 A.M. and log the returns, which would come at erratic intervals throughout the morning.

It was the type of job that alternates between frenetic activity and slack periods, and during the slack periods—when I had the office to myself—I would practice singing, sometimes simply vocalizing scales but occasionally belting out an aria.

In addition to the produce market, Covent Garden is the site of Covent Garden Opera House—London's equivalent to the San Carlos Opera House in Naples. The rehearsal rooms overlooked the market, and each afternoon, the voices of the world's greatest divas, tenors, and basses would drift through the now-quiet produce facilities. After work, I would stand beneath the window of whatever rehearsal room was producing the most exciting sounds, listening. It was like being on Gigli's doorstep again, so close and yet so far! My singing career would eventually put me in some of the world's finest venues, but the closest I would ever get to singing in Covent Garden would be in the empties manager's office.

• • •

Sometimes, I had the money for voice training. My teacher was Harold Miller, who worked out of a private rehearsal facility comprised of 40 or so practice rooms. Between lessons, I still wanted to practice but had trouble raising cash for room rental.

I had moved from Covent Garden to an office job with the Automobile Association, where singing at work wasn't acceptable behavior. The office was close to the studio, though, and during lunch hour there was time to skip over to it for a bit of practice. Room rentals were by the hour, and it had occurred to me that some musicians probably left without using their full time. So I would cruise the halls, looking for abandoned rooms where I might catch a few minutes of practice without paying. I wasn't the only singer doing so; there were several of us who cheated regularly on room rental because we were so poor.

One day, one of the paying customers told me of a job opening, cleaning passenger carriages for the Southern Railway at nearly double the pay I was getting from the Automobile Association. The extra cash allowed me to become a legitimate paying guest at the studio, but the job itself also gave me its own practice venue with certain unique advantages. The railway was sprucing up its entire line of rolling stock, and my task was to coat the exterior of the carriages in a gelatinous concoction of some kind of acid. I never knew exactly what was in it and am probably happier not knowing. After I had liberally coated each carriage with the mystery substance, the car would be shunted into an enormous washing shed. When it emerged, it had shed years of accumulated grime and was ready for repainting.

The gel was applied outdoors, where fumes were at a minimum, but sometimes I was assigned to indoor work, stripping off old paint and varnish. It was a tedious and mind-numbing job, but the sheds had wonderful acoustics, with excellent reverberation. To distract myself, I often sang. The result was impressive—like singing in a shower, only more so. Soon I was belting out "O Sole Mio" or some aria I had been working on in my lessons.

On more than one occasion, the cockney foreman would gruffly pretend to take me task. "Hey, w'ere d'ya fink you are, bloody Covent Garden?" he would ask. "Git on wiv' it, mate." Eventually I informed him that I had, in my own way, already sung there. But this was better yet. The high metal ceilings and walls of these sheds made me sound like the great tenors I was trying to emulate. The foreman was a humorous and generally benign character who would often greet me at the start of our day with, "Wot bloody song are ya gonna' grace us wiv' today, mate?" He secretly enjoyed my singing and was visibly moved when I gave notice several months later that an audition had come through and I would be leaving for a theatrical tour.

## Going for It: Houston—January 15, 1995

Part of preparing for a marathon is carbohydrate loading and maintaining good hydration. Needless to say, these are not compatible with diarrhea. With each dash for the bathroom, I could feel my strength diminishing, even as I swallowed antidiarrheal pills, uncountable glasses of water, and digestion-friendly plain, dry bagels. For four weeks, I had devoted all of my time and energy to preparing for this race. Now I was busier than ever, trying not to lose too much ground.

Nine other runners were similarly afflicted. We commiserated among ourselves while the race officials apologized and wrung their hands. Then came the morning of the race. I felt better and was beginning to think I still had a chance.

My plan had been to start at a 6:45 pace, even though a three-hour marathon is actually seven seconds per mile slower. That was because I was after two records that day: the marathon and the U.S. 30K record, which would be officially scored at the 30K split.

The first part of the race went according to plan. I crossed the 30K mark nicely ahead of the older record. Of course, it wasn't really a U.S. record because, although I had applied for American citizenship, I was still a British citizen. It might have been a British record, but I never found out.

My 30K time was 2:07:05—a 6:49 pace. That put me 40 seconds ahead of three-hour pace and a minute and a half ahead of Warren Utes's world-record pace. Surprisingly, I still felt strong.

Then, suddenly, I fell apart. I had slowed down before during my 30-plus prior marathons, but never before had I hit the wall. Now, I hit it with such a resounding thump that I was shocked beyond belief. Practically from one minute to the next, my legs turned to jelly and my whole body rejected the effort.

I was dismayed, but at least I knew the problem wasn't the fault of my training or race plan. The diarrhea had obviously kept me from properly carboloading, and now my muscles had simply run out of fuel. My pace slowed by nearly two minutes per mile, and I struggled to the finish in 3:14:25.

Still, I knew I wasn't about to give up. Even before I had showered away the last of my sweat, I knew where I would make my next attempt. A few weeks before, I had been invited to the world's first age-graded marathon, in Valencia, Spain. I had even been offered one thousand dollars in travel expenses and a chance of winning more than that in prize money. There were only three weeks between Houston and Valencia—in theory, not enough time to recover, let alone retrain. But by sapping my energy the way it had, my illness may have kept me from beating up my muscles the way you usually do in a marathon. If so, I would bounce back quickly.

I called the Spanish officials and told them I was accepting their offer.

## *Down Argentina Way*: London—Circa 1952

Working in theater, you quickly learn to handle onstage disasters. In the mid-1960s, I was in a touring revue called *Down Argentina Way*, which (as the title indicates) featured South American music, dance, and comedy sketches. My voice and "movement" were good enough that I was hired as lead singer for several of the production numbers. Dance was never my forte, but with many hours of practice, I managed to cope with the choreography reasonably well. On tour, we did eight shows a week: nightly performances every day but Sunday, plus matinees on Wednesdays and Saturdays. Part of my job was to keep the audience entertained during a major scene change midway through the show. That type of entertaining is a lost art with today's revolving stages, but it was an important part of keeping the show from losing momentum. It was also a chance to sing a few solos of my own choice.

My accompaniment for these songs was the theater orchestra, which was a local ensemble retained by each theater we visited. Usually, these orchestras were fine, but some were a trifle wanting, making the entire revue a bit . . . challenging. Perhaps the tempo would be too fast and we would try to speed up to match it or, failing that, try to get the orchestra to change tempo by changing the pace of our singing or dancing.

Normally, I sang two songs, "Charmaine" and "Santa Lucia." But in one theater in a western suburb of London, the managers wanted more time between the matinee and the evening performance. The show had been receiving glowing write-ups in the local press, and large crowds were making it hard to get the afternoon audience out on schedule and the evening audience in. To save a bit of time, the stage crews scurried extra-fast through the set change, and we decided to cut the first number, "Charmaine," from the lineup.

Everything went fine during the matinee. In the evening, the house was packed and the audience was the most receptive of the week. We in the cast reciprocated, and I myself was in especially fine voice. Everything was going (as we like to say in England) swimmingly.

Then came my solos.

This orchestra had been one of the good ones, and there had been no problems to date. But as I stepped onto the apron to sing, it failed to produce either "Charmaine" or "Santa Lucia." Rather, I was greeted by a dissonant noise unlike anything I had ever heard before.

Panic does not begin to describe the way I felt. Like a performer's worst nightmare, I stood frozen in front of a packed house, with no clue what to do. *Disaster, disaster, disaster* flashed a warning buzzer in my mind, like an air-raid siren. But there was nowhere to flee.

*Star Trek* had not yet started appearing on the airwaves, or "Beam me up, Scotty" might have crossed my mind. Instead, I just wished there were some way to magically disappear.

So there I stood: black flamenco pants, a beautiful white blouse, bouffant sleeves, a large, open collar, and a broad red cummerbund around my waist. I was the perfect picture of the Latin singer (however English I might be)—with nothing to sing. I spread my arms wide, in what to me was a hopeless gesture of "Excuse me, folks." To my surprise, it garnered enthusiastic applause. Then, at last, the familiar strains of my first song came from the orchestra pit, and I was back in my element. I cast a quick glance to the conductor, who was beaming and nodding to me, mouthing his agreement that yes, we were indeed back on track.

The adrenaline surge injected a brilliance into my voice such as was rarely there, and for a brief moment, I felt like the finest tenor in the world, my high notes resounding through the auditorium back to me. I gave both songs everything I had, wishing I had a whole recital to perform because I might never sing this well again. Then it was over, and the applause seemed thunderous, though that too might have been the adrenaline. Acknowledging the conductor, I took a bow and made my exit, happy to have escaped from this fiasco and amazed at how well I had sung once the cacophony had cleared.

Afterward, the conductor was all apologies. After the change in lineup for the matinee, he said, he had forgotten to tell the orchestra that both songs were again planned for the evening. Half of them figured it out and started the first song, while the other half assumed we were doing the same thing we had done in the afternoon and started the second.

My panicked shrug had saved the day, but afterward, one of our comedians, experienced in the art of the ad lib, said I could have done even better by turning dramatically to the orchestra and saying: "Excuse me, Mr. Conductor, but I'm going *Down Argentina Way*. Might I ask which way you're going?" Of course, if I could have done that on a moment's notice, I would have been a comic rather than a singer.

# CHAPTER 6

# Orange Blossoms

## Valencia, Spain—February 5, 1995

Animo! Animo! *"Go, go, go!"* Fuerza, Ale!

*The shouts of encouragement broke against me like warm Mediterranean waves. I was living a dream almost unimaginable to a runner of my age: leading a field of two thousand through the streets of Valencia, Spain, toward a finish line in the local stadium.*

• • •

I recovered quickly from my poor finish in Houston. There were only three weeks to train for my next marathon, so I gave myself four days' rest and then ran 12 miles at a 7:20 pace. The next day, I ran ten 400-meter repeats on the track. On the following three days, I ran a total of 30 miles, including a 14-miler at only a few seconds slower than my desired marathon pace. The next three days I rested (if traveling to London and then to Spain can be considered resting).

In Valencia I did a few interviews, then was whisked off to a resort 50 miles south of the city, where I engaged in one of the world's best cures for jet lag: a half-hour jog along a beautiful beach. To one side were the blue waters of the Mediterranean. To the other, the sun sank orange-yellow behind high mountains. The air was scented with the perfume of orange blossoms. Whatever might happen in the race, I was glad to be here.

• • •

*As I passed the 20K mark, I grabbed a bottle of water. I had been on the course for nearly 85 minutes now, and the kilometers were ticking away in a steady 4 minute, 12 second rhythm, a 6:45 mile pace. I felt good: smooth and comfortable. The weather had been chilly at the start, but a quilt of thoughts had warmed me as I remembered all of the other races that had gone so well in the 15 years I had been running. Houston was an anomaly. I was back in my element: relaxed, confident, and in charge of my own body.*

*I was also running alone, just behind the pace car, flanked by a police escort. Nobody my age had ever before had such an experience. It was both exhilarating and intimidating.*

• • •

I spent a week making final preparations and enjoying the seaside resort. With seven days to go, I did my last long run, an easy 15.5 miles along a country road lined by orange groves. One boyhood Christmas, I had found one of these Valencia oranges in my stocking, wrapped in tissue paper with gold lettering. The orange was a treat but the paper a treasure that spoke of exotic climes far beyond my London home. I kept it for months and then added it to a collection of other children's souvenirs on a bulletin board in my school's geography room.

Lost in the memory, I ran faster than intended. The next day I held the distance to 6 miles, but three of them were again faster than planned: 6:34 per mile. I was more than ready to race again, even though Houston had been so very, very recent.

Tuesday before the race was my last significant workout: a three-kilometer warm-up followed by 1,000-meter repeats at paces dropping from 4:50 to 3:36 (6:34 to 5:48 per mile). The workout was designed as a final bit of speed sharpening, but it had another purpose, too. In U.S. races, courses are marked in miles. In Europe, they're marked in kilometers. To the extent possible, by race day, I wanted to be thinking in kilometers.

On Wednesday, I walked two kilometers in the morning and three in the evening. Then I finished my training with an easy six kilometers on Thursday, after which my wife, sister, and I drove to Valencia for dinner with members of the Correcaminos running club, the sponsor of the upcoming race. At a café overlooking the Mediterranean, we enjoyed the best paella I had ever eaten, presented as a work of art in a large, round shallow pan held high above our table by the chef—the type of presentation that draws applause even before you've tasted it. This was carboloading at its finest. Too bad it didn't have a wrapper I could save, like my Valencia orange!

Friday was also relaxed, eating carbohydrates and keeping my legs elevated as much as possible. The goal of resting in this manner is to make you feel energized and strong. It was working. I was hungry to run.

• • •

*Valencia is a bustling city of a half million, with a nice mix of modernity and Old World charm. Streets range from boulevards to narrow alleys with buildings crammed tightly together above them. Luckily, the racecourse stuck to the wider streets.*

*I had never before previewed a marathon course, and it seemed bad luck to do so this time, but I knew I would be leading the pack and was afraid of getting lost. What an ignoble end to my second attempt at the record if I strayed off course and disqualified myself! That would be worse than the food poisoning because it would be my own fault.*

*The race officials assured me there was no need to worry. All 42 kilometers of the course would be marked with a continuous blue line. The pace car would know the way. There was no way that I could accidentally wander off course. Still, I memorized the route's twistings and turnings. It started on a side street near a big supermarket, Continente, a major sponsor. From there, it followed a boulevard for two kilometers and then turned toward the center of the city, passing several impressive monuments. At the six-kilometer mark, it dropped 10 meters into a short tunnel beneath another road. Climbing back out of the tunnel was the biggest hill of an otherwise very flat course.*

*From the tunnel, the route ran along a dry riverbed. The river had been diverted in the 1950s to alleviate flooding, and its bed was now a greenway with gardens, parks, running trails, tennis courts, and the stadium where, after several more meanders, we would finish.*

• • •

All of the officials of the Correcaminos club knew my goal: I had told them when I had accepted their invitation to participate in the race. One of the men who had invited me, Paco Borao, served as my interpreter and mother hen. He told me to treat the race as a training run, that whatever I did would be fine. But the newspapers had the story and were listing me as a favorite not only to set my record, but to win the entire race.

The format was different from anything I had ever experienced before. Runners would start in waves, oldest first, handicapped according to the differences in pace predicted by the WAVA tables. I was in the oldest group, comprised of only four runners. We would start 46 minutes and 10 seconds ahead of the young elites. The marathon had been run without age grading for 14 years, and the open-class record was 2:14:28. If I could run 3:00:37, no young elite could beat me without setting a course record.

Newspapers nationwide were picking up the story, carrying photos and articles about a John Keston who seemed increasingly alien to me. I was also increasingly aware of the race's prize money, which would be awarded not by raw finishing time but according to the age-graded scores: two thousand dollars for first, one thousand dollars for second, and five hundred dollars for third. In some of my earlier marathons, back in the United States, math whizzes had calculated that on an age-graded system, I would have been the overall winner. Then, I had merely been amused. Now, I realized, I had the chance not only to do precisely that but to graduate to the ranks of professional athletes.

I was drawing a lot of attention as the oldest contender with a chance of winning. But the papers seemed to have forgotten that there were good masters runners from Russia, Switzerland, England, Morocco, Portugal, Sweden, Germany, and Spain in younger age groups. They too got handicaps, though not as big as mine. I would get a head start on them, but could I maintain it?

• • •

Following the paella dinner, I had moved into a downtown hotel. At 7:30 on race day morning—a Saturday in this Catholic country—Paco met me in the lobby and then walked me to the starting line, a few blocks away. It was cold—48 degrees—and I walked to warm up before shifting to my usual stretching routine. Paco sensed my nervousness and, ignoring the 20-year age difference, put his arm around me as though I were the youngster, telling me again that nobody expected anything more from me than I was capable of on that day. "You'll do well," he added.

His words settled me, and I began to think constructively about the task ahead. Then, a bit after 8:30 A.M., the other 70-year-olds and I began the race. Immediately I went into the lead: a new experience. Ahead was the pace car, around me an escort of police on motorcycles. Spectators were everywhere, and someone in the pace car was using a loudspeaker, calling out my name and age and asking the crowds to "put palms together for applause!"

At every corner, crossroad, and turning, the invocation rang out: "Here is John Keston! Applaud! Applaud!" As an actor, I was accustomed to applause but not to this extended ovation that flowed ahead of me. It was energizing, and I hit the first kilometer mark in 4:06 (a 6:36 pace), about six seconds faster than intended.

I should have worked then to tame the adrenaline and take control of my pace, but I was running smoothly, feeling no stress or pressure. The kilometers flitted by and I continued to be buoyed by the encouragement of the crowds.

*Animo, animo! Fuerza.* "Go, go, go!" I had expected leading a race to be a lonely experience, but it wasn't. With the blue line to follow, a pace car, the press van, and a police escort, I was most definitely not alone.

As the kilometers fell beneath my feet, I kept thinking about the finish. *What would it be like entering the stadium?* I couldn't imagine stepping into it alone and in the lead, and yet that was indeed a prospect. I pushed such thoughts out of my head and concentrated on sustaining the pace that might bring them to fruition.

•  •  •

*When I had drunk as much as I could from the 20-kilometer water bottle, I followed the blue line around a corner and tossed the bottle and its remaining contents toward the sidewalk. It was a casual decision, the type of thing I was accustomed to doing at aid stations in prior marathons: drink what you want now . . . get more later. It had worked well for eight prior sub-three-hour marathons, and I gave it no thought today. But not much later, I would be wishing I could have back the water I had so casually discarded.*

•  •  •

Paco had told me the race was being run in strict adherence to the rules and regulations of the Association of International Marathons and Road Races. One of these rules was that water tables were to be placed every five kilometers—not once a mile, as in many U.S. races. In addition to water, these tables would carry a sports drink. In the United States, there were several brands that I had used on occasion. Here in Spain, the offering was Isostar, a European beverage I had never heard of before.

Because I was not yet feeling stressed, it had not occurred to me to take two water bottles off a table and carry the second until I was ready for it. I had also underestimated how quickly this dry, sunny climate could warm up.

Forty-eight degrees at the start did not mean 58 degrees or even 68 at the finish. By the time my three hours were up, it would be 80 degrees.

At the half-marathon mark, I was still on track for a sub-3:00, though I was beginning to notice the heat. At kilometer 25, I drank everything I could, not wasting water by throwing it away. That which I couldn't drink I poured over my head. By the next aid station, at kilometer 30, I was still moving well but had slowed from a 4:12-per-kilometer pace to 4:18 (6:55 per mile). I could still break three hours, but it was getting progressively hotter.

It still did not occur to me to take two water bottles and carry one farther along the course. Much of running is the accumulation of habits: habits of stride and arm carriage, habits of breathing and prerace stretching and finding the rhythms at which you can run for hours, seemingly on autopilot but actually (and habitually) checking the details to make sure the autopilot is functioning correctly. Now, one of my habits was threatening to undo me. Also, I was afraid to touch the Isostar. Research has shown that the sugar in sports drinks can help in the later stages of the race, but race day is an extremely dangerous time to try a new concoction. It might work . . . or it might give you diarrhea.

As the race progressed, the crowds grew. The cheers became louder and kept me running as well as I could, even though I was beginning to have doubts.

• • •

At kilometer 35, I was still leading, but my legs were feeling heavy and I was losing pace. I had slipped to a 5:00 kilometer (8:03 per mile), and between kilometer 39 and kilometer 40—less than two miles from the finish—I was forced to walk for about 30 meters. At the final aid station, at kilometer 40, the equivalent of mile 25, I didn't just grab a water bottle on the run, I stopped for a full 30 or 40 seconds to drink it.

I was still leading, but my concern now was simply to finish.

I was wearing a heart rate monitor, and I had taken those two breaks because my heart rate was hitting 155—pretty close to my maximum. If I kept that up, I would collapse from fatigue in the final mile—a fate that has been met by more than a few marathoners. Thanks to the breaks, my heart rate fell to 146, and I knew that I could finish, but not nearly as well as I had hoped.

I was still determined not to let down my new friends of the Correcaminos club. I gutted out the final two kilometers, but with one kilometer to go, a

40-year-old Russian named Yuri Mikhailov passed me. Despite the heat, he looked very strong.

Surprisingly, I wasn't discouraged. Even though I had given up on my record and had now lost the win, I knew that on this scorchingly hot day I was on the verge of posting one of the two or three fastest marathon times ever recorded by a 70-year-old. I would not disappoint the good people of Valencia.

When I finally entered the stadium, I couldn't believe the reception. The entire arena chanted, "Keston! Keston! Keston!" It was the biggest thrill of my entire running career.

I hit the track three hundred meters from the finish. By now, I was lumbering, my torso flagging and pitching ahead, a far cry from the elegant, upright stance of the comfortable, seemingly fresh finisher. One hundred meters later, I had another swing of emotion. Among the overwhelming cheers, I said, quite loudly to myself, "God, there's still two hundred meters to go!"

I crossed the line nearly doubled over with fatigue. Paco caught me before I could fall. I was in second place overall, with a respectable 3:02:50. It age-adjusted to 2:16:40, which put me 1:45 behind Mikhailov's adjusted time of 2:14:55. Third place would go to a 31-year-old Swede who didn't take kindly to being beaten by a 70-year-old.

• • •

To this point, I had been focused entirely on my race and was unprepared for what was in store for me at the finish. I was immediately surrounded by photographers, reporters, and fans wanting autographs. Parents asked me to pose with their children. Then I was plucked out of this maelstrom and ushered away to another new experience: drug testing.

Once all the runners were in, awards were presented by the mayor of Valencia herself. Even though I was only second—and had not achieved my record—I was given an enormous silver cup, 19 inches tall and a foot across at the top. I couldn't help but wonder how it would fit into the overhead luggage compartment on the flight home. But there was more to come. At a postrace celebration that evening, the Correcaminos club presented me with a separate award, another silver cup nearly as large as the first. And there was also an age-group award and a finisher's medal. Four awards for one race seemed a bit over the top, and that wasn't even counting the one thousand dollars, which would be sent following a satisfactory result on the drug test.

I had missed my record, but not by much. In the heat, I didn't really have much to complain about except the paucity of aid stations and my brain-dead failure to recognize that I could carry a water bottle with me. I had also let the excitement draw me out too fast. Had those first few kilometers been just slightly slower—4:12s rather than 4:06s—I would have been 90 seconds slower at the 15-kilometer mark and probably a lot faster at the finish.

Next time, I figured, I would go somewhere cooler—and where I could drink a bit more often than every five kilometers. I would also go out at a more conservative pace.

# CHAPTER 7

# In the Zone

## MGM Records: London—1954

For several years, life as an aspiring singer/actor continued. I collected more minor roles in musicals but was still looking for something that would showcase me as an individual performer. Meanwhile, the process was putting a strain on my marriage. Mariolina hadn't signed on to be the wife of a penniless actor.

When I finally got a break, it came, as such things are prone to do, by surprise and in roundabout fashion. It started when, looking for a chance to do something different, I volunteered to perform at the Nufield Center.

The center was a multipurpose facility for the entertainment of British troops on leave, somewhat like a community recreation center. From the military's perspective, it served as a place where soldiers, sailors, and airmen could spend their leave time happy, pleasantly occupied, and out of trouble. From the soldiers' perspective, it was a place to meet girls—either civilians or fellow members of the armed services—and to play snooker, billiards, darts, and card games.

In addition to game facilities, the center had a cafeteria and a stage where artists, some famous, some not, entertained free of charge, often testing material for new acts. I was in the not-famous category, but the center allotted me 12 minutes of performance time as part of a concert with several other performers.

Twelve minutes is time enough for four or five songs. I had plenty of material, but since my goal was diversification, I went in search of new pieces. One goal was to find something I could hone for an audition with Phillips Records, then a young label always looking for new talent.

One of the pieces I had decided to perform was Mario Lanza's "Because You're Mine," which was popular because Lanza's movie, *The Great Caruso*, was currently in the cinemas. Also, long before, a friend had told me you never know who might be in the audience, so it's always wise to have some material that shows you at your best. "Because You're Mine" was the type of song that would show off my bright tenor sound, so I went to the publisher's office to get a promotional copy of the music.

The clerk brought me the music and then asked if I would like to give it a try.

"Certainly," I said.

He disappeared into a back room and then returned with a bespectacled gentleman in a tweed jacket. "This is Wilfred Burns," he said. "He's a song-writer and conductor. He says he'd be happy to accompany you."

I later learned that Wilfred wasn't merely "a" songwriter and conductor; he was one of some renown who just happened to be at the publisher's, show-ing some recent compositions. But at the moment, I knew him merely as a gracious gentleman who was doing me a favor.

With Wilfred accompanying me, I easily sang "Because You're Mine." But the published key was lower than necessary for my voice, and I could take the high notes several steps higher. By now, I had even mastered the dreaded high C, though I had heard it suggested that you have only a limited number of those in your life, so you had better use them sparingly. I'm not sure that's true, but maybe it's like racing: sometimes it's wise to save the all-out efforts for when you need them.

In this case, however, the published version didn't even come close to a high C, and Wilfred agreed I could do better. Sight reading, he transposed the song a tone and a half higher, and I sang again, my high notes resounding mellifluous and strong.

"You have a great sound," Wilfred said, after we ended on a splendid high G.

A moment later, the door opened from the back room. "Was that you?" asked a tall man about my age. I admitted that it was, and he introduced himself as John something-or-other—Michelson, I think, but even though it proved to be one of the most important meetings of my life, time has mysteriously swallowed his last name.

"Why do you want that song?" he asked.

I told him about the concert and my hope of using the piece to audition for Phillips.

He looked me over in an odd, summing-up manner that made me feel very much on display. "Do you have any other music with you?"

I nodded. By chance, I was carrying the music for a song about a part of Naples called Marechiare. The name means "clear sea," and the song tells of how moonlight is so enchanting that even the little fish want love. Perhaps not the perfect song, but it was what I had available, and my performance of it always benefited from my love of all things Neapolitan.

Wilfred took one look at the music and sight read it perfectly, even though it was a song he had never even heard before. He truly was an astounding accompanist, and I was beginning to get a glimmer that he might be considerably more. When I ended on a resounding high A, everyone in the office applauded, including Michelson.

Grinning now, he told me why he had wanted me to sing again. "I'm the artiste and repertoire agent for MGM Records," he said. "How about auditioning for us, rather than Phillips?" He added that I had exactly the kind of voice that he was looking for and that I was a good-looking chap with the sort of figure the girls would swoon over. My friend had certainly been correct when he advised me to always prepare every performance under the presumption that someone unexpected might be listening in. I had just never anticipated that the unexpected might occur at a practice session.

• • •

Two days later, I was at the Abbey Road recording studio in London (later made famous by the Beatles) for a formal audition. I passed with flying colors and shortly after received a telegram from John telling me that yes, we were going to make a record and that I was to be treated as the next great star-in-the-making.

The following two weeks were unbelievably exciting. I had been in show business for years, but I was having trouble keeping track of what was real. Indeed, the entire string of events seemed like utter fantasy. A couple of days after I received John's telegram, he, Wilfred, and I returned to the music publisher's office, this time as colleagues. I had canceled the Nufield Center concert and dropped my plans to learn "Because You're Mine." John was looking for previously unrecorded music, and that piece was anything but new. We needed two songs, and eventually we picked English translations of "Mardi Gras" and "There Was a Time," the latter by a French composer named Charles Trenet. I was to be accompanied by a 40-piece orchestra, which Wilfred would conduct. Wilfred would also arrange the music for strings, woodwinds, brass, and percussion and took me into his home for daily rehearsals.

Just the idea of performing before a full orchestra gave me shivers of anticipation. I had never sung with any accompaniment larger than a theater orchestra, typically about a dozen instruments. Now, I would be accompanied by 40 of the finest musicians in London. It was all becoming more exciting by the moment, but also scarier. Would I be able to do it justice?

## Hayward Field Poetry: Eugene, Oregon—2001

Every runner has a few perfect races where everything works—like making music at its finest. One of mine came years after my marathon quest and stands like one of those idyllic memories on stage—the running equivalent of practicing and performing before Wilfred's orchestra.

Hayward Field is one of the most famous racing venues in North America. It was here that coach Bill Bowerman tested the world's first "waffle" treaded shoes—homemade in his wife's waffle iron. Here, greats like Steve Prefontaine, Alberto Salazar, and Mary Slaney helped make Eugene into "Track Town, USA." It is a place where every step echoes of history.

Each year, the university hosts the Hayward Masters Classic, a two-day meet limited to older athletes, with five-year age divisions all the way up to 95-plus.

The previous three running years had not been good to me. The second winter after my hip repair, I slipped on some ice and broke my fibula. Coming back from that, I tripped over a rock while trail running and tore up my foot. Three injuries, three recoveries, three lost years. Now, finally, I was back in business. My goal was the 75–79 age-division world record for 10,000 meters.

The time to beat was 42:03, set in 1989 by an Englishman named David Morrison. In preparation, I had run three 10K road races in the previous six months, whittling my time from a post-winter-hibernation 47:41 to 43:20, still well shy of Morrison's mark.

Preparing for an important race is a form of theater, performed to an audience of one. Like good theater, it has rhythm and poetry. The rhythm comes from the workouts, which cycle through a hard-easy pattern as you alternately tax the muscles, then let them recover, again and again. The poetry comes from merging all the factors necessary for a good performance: nutrition, training, racing schedules, and the all-important endeavor known as "peaking." Along with this comes a sort of duet between opposing pieces of your mind, beginning with the sweet seduction of "Could I?" in counterpoint to the more realistic tones of "Should I?" then maturing into the back-and-forth tones of "I will" and the minor-key tremors of "It'll never work."

Ten thousand meters is 25 laps. To make the record, I merely needed to run a whisker more than three seconds per lap faster than my pace on the road. Put that way, it seemed easy. After all, three seconds isn't much. *I can handle that*, I thought.

•   •   •

The 10,000 was the meet's first event, scheduled for 8:30 A.M., an hour before the official opening ceremonies. Leaving home at dawn, I drove south through the June greenery of Oregon's Willamette Valley. The farms and fields were a perfect balm for my doubts, and I reached the track at 7:30.

I was two laps into a planned two-mile warm-up when the doubts struck. In addition to the expected jumble of nerves and butterflies were doubts about my warm-up routine itself. *I would be running 25 circuits of this course during the race*, I thought. *Maybe I shouldn't be running eight of them now.*

If there's any single rule of racing, it's that changing plans on race day is almost always a bad idea. Your conscious brain thinks it's in control, but actually, it's the doubts that are now in command. So I resisted the temptation to cut short my jog. Instead, I tried to think of the race in artistic terms. Before singing a concert, performing an operatic role, or acting in a play, I would run through each melody, vocal phrase, text, or scene, repeating important lines and notes several times. Here, my rehearsal room was different, but the need was the same. As I encountered other runners, I cast them as actors, each of us part of the same production. I nodded to acquaintances but kept mostly to myself. The rest of the cast was unaware of my intent, and I was happy to keep it that way.

A cool breeze was blowing from the southwest, and I was comfortable jogging in sweats. Few spectators watch an early-morning 10,000, and the stadium was quiet, affording me a mental therapy I had not expected. Except for the normal elevation of my pulse rate from my warm-up, I was relaxed, at peace with what would follow. The stage was set, my rehearsal complete.

It was a beautiful morning, with wisps of cloud gliding between sun breaks now warming our bodies. The changing light highlighted the other runners, with their colored shorts and singlets, impressing me not only with the beauty of the day but also with the beauties of the human form and the spirit of competition. I was ready to run my best. And running my best, I reminded myself, was all that I could ever ask of myself.

## Meet John Keston: London—1955

For most people, especially men, a name is something you're born with and keep throughout your life. Women may change surnames when they're married, but few normally change both their first and last names.

Not so with performers. Not only do we put on new characters for each role, but sometimes we're asked to assume new identities for ourselves, as well.

In 1955, it was time to bid adieu to Frank Caston. A few days before the MGM recording session, sitting in a café, John Michelson gave me the news.

"You've got to change your name," he said, "You need something more euphonious."

"What's wrong with Frank?" I had been Frank for 30 years and couldn't imagine anything else, not to mention that it was my father's name. Throwing it away seemed disrespectful.

"It's that *KK* sound," he said. "It's too harsh. And hard to pronounce clearly. Say it quickly and it comes up as Fran Caston."

I sipped my tea. It was made in the British way, strong, with milk and sugar—powerful tea, just as there was power to the name Frank. Just as there was class to the name Francis. When I had performed under a different name before, it had been to protect that name, not avoid it.

Still, I wanted to be a success and definitely not as somebody whose name was always mispronounced. "What would you recommend?" I asked.

We batted names around for a half hour, with no consensus. Some of Michelson's ideas weren't bad, but none felt like *me*. By the time my tea was gone, though, I was resigned to the fact that my life as Frank had disappeared with it. Then my eye fell on a manila envelope containing a musical arrangement I had had done for me sometime earlier. Someone had written my name on it, but had misspelled it as Keston.

*Keston*, I thought. *That's not bad. I could see myself as Keston.*

I pointed it out to John, who quickly agreed. He liked the *K*, which carried more strength than the *C*. Yes, he said, Keston was very good, but not if I remained Frank, because it only accented the problem with the double *K*. "But the first name needs to be strong and very English," he added.

He, of course, had clear ideas about what is the strongest, most English name of all. From that moment on, we were both John.

When I told her, Mariolina wasn't happy, though she was somewhat mollified when I said that she and the boys didn't need to change their names. Years later, when Tony followed in my footsteps and took up marathon running in his fifties, we ran a few races together. The father-son team of Keston and Caston must have confused people, but nobody asked. In running, unlike theater, it really doesn't matter whether your name is properly euphonious or even whether anyone can pronounce it. I've heard many an ethnic name slaughtered at award ceremonies or in races where the announcer calls out everyone's name as he or she crosses the finish, but a personal best is still a personal best, even if the announcer mangles your name.

In many ways, the name change to Keston was a rite of passage. You need to have achieved a certain degree of success to warrant a new name, and I took it as a benchmark. I was by no means old, but I was no longer a kid, either. It would be years before I adopted the name John Keston for my private life—now it even adorns my passport—but publicly, I had made the change. Frank was the kid. John would be the adult.

• • •

"John Keston" was now ready for his recording session. Abbey Road was an immense facility, as large as a concert hall, with all the latest equipment. It was where symphonies made their recordings.

I was in awe the moment I stepped in the door. Dozens of microphones were scattered around the recording area, and the technicians had used an eight-foot screen to build me a three-sided ministudio where I could sing, protected from the massive sounds of the orchestra. I had a window, so I could see the conductor, and my own microphone, allowing the engineers to mix the sound so that my voice would rise above the entire ensemble. It was all very flattering.

I was thoroughly prepped and thoroughly focused, and the nerves that had nearly defeated me in my audition with Professor Morelli were, thankfully, nowhere to be found.

As the musicians filtered in, I warmed up with Wilfred, running through last-minute rehearsals of both songs. In the background, the orchestra was soon doing the same, filling this enormous hall with its lush sound. It was hard to believe that all of this was for me. On most occasions I would have felt intimidated—wondering whether I truly deserved this—but for once, rather than stage fright, what I felt was thrilled.

Then it was time to sing. My voice rose to the occasion, and the performance felt solid. We did several takes until the engineers were satisfied and then it was over. The entire thing lasted about 90 minutes, but I was so deeply involved in what I was doing that I had no recollection of how long it took.

Runners have a term for the perfect race: they refer to it as being "in the zone." It's a state of heightened alertness and total concentration in which you are so involved in what you are doing that there is no time for self-doubt. Afterward, even elite runners will often be startled by the outcome, telling their coaches that it felt too easy—as though they weren't actually working. At Abbey Road, I was in the zone as a performer. It was an extraordinary experience.

## Hayward Field Poetry, Verse 2: Eugene, Oregon— 2001

There were only 20 other runners in the 10,000 meters—too few to split into separate heats, so I would be running with all of the others, including the 40-year-olds. That was fine by me; the younger runners would pull me along with them. Perhaps I could float like the wispy clouds, or like Muhammad Ali, like a butterfly. No need to sting like a bee: I was the only one in my age group and bound to win.

We were called to the starting line, and the officials positioned me to the outside of the track. I would have rather been on the inside, but as long as you don't get boxed into an outer lane on the turn, it's not a big difference.

The gun set us off, and immediately, several runners surged ahead of me. Crossing behind them, I took eighth position, following a 50-year-old I knew I could beat. My plan was to run an even pace at one hundred seconds per lap—enough to break Morrison's record by three seconds. But I got pulled out too fast around the first lap, and as I went by, my lap counter—a race official whom I had informed of my goal—shouted, "Eighty-nine seconds!"

I dropped my pace to 98 seconds for the second lap but still passed the 50-year-old, who had overextended himself far worse than I had.

Slowly, I began to settle in, trying to find that sweet, comfortable sensation that comes from running with relaxed confidence. But the stress was still there at the end of the eighth lap. *Oh, my*! I thought. Seventeen more to go. I was still ahead of pace, but I had the nagging feeling that I should keep doing 98s in case, later on, I tired and fell off pace. In fact, I was already losing ground because I had clocked laps six and seven at 101 seconds each—a second slower than planned.

And then, my internal coach and strategist was swallowed up by the here and now.

*Can I get more comfortable yet*? I think. *Well, of course*! It often happens like magic after two to two and a half miles. The body becomes a machine, ticking over meticulously as the laps clip by. The mind runs free. The legs become lighter and almost senseless. On television, we see the airiness of the world's great runners—how they fairly glide over the ground. At 76, I am no longer flowing as they did, but the sensation is still splendid.

The sun peeks through as I run on the back straight. It warms my back and legs. I have moved into fifth position, and I have only three and one-half laps to go. My thoughts jumble and flit through the incredible orchestrations necessary for bringing the race together—the intricacies of organizing, starting, and timing the meet, the need to have enough officials to watch every athlete so that nobody breaks a rule. It's part of the poetry of a great track meet. But my own job is simple, and my legs keep turning over, onward, inevitably toward the finish. It is a beautiful experience made more memorable by the sweetness of the morning air and the quiet of an almost spectatorless arena. Nobody else in the world is running at world-record pace at this very instant. I understand the uniqueness of the moment and let it envelop me.

The lap counter breaks my reverie by reminding me, with three laps to go, that I need to hit at least 102 seconds apiece. I had lost two seconds on the preceding lap and am still not totally confident. So many things can yet go wrong, but my task is simple: keep the machine in gear and continue going around and around.

It is only on the last lap, when I see the big digital clock on the score-board at the end of the field, that I really believe I can get the record. I glance up and there it is: 40:18. Amazingly, I can still do math. I'm on pace. All I have to do is another of those 101-second laps and I'll not only get the record but break 42 minutes while I'm at it. *Play it cool*, I think. *It's too far to sprint.*

But I have tired more than expected, and I lose precious seconds on the back straight. Then I enter the final curve, locally known as Bowerman Corner. I reach as deep as I can and summon what passes for a kick as the finish line stretches agonizingly ahead. And then I am across, wheezing and looking desperately for the clock. And there it is: 41:59.08. The meet officials know what that means, and shortly afterward they are telling everyone over the loudspeakers. The record has fallen, and it is mine, but sweet as it feels, I am still lost in the poetry of those middle laps, when everything worked without conscious thought.

• • •

The meet formally began 20 minutes later. I love to sing the national anthem at races and was scheduled to do so here, but it's one thing to sing before a race and quite another to sing so shortly after. I was a little dismayed by how many stairs I had to climb to get to the microphone. Here was the new world record holder panting and puffing his way to the booth—although it was partly my fault for trying to run up the stairs—and I had to ask for a brief respite to catch my breath. Then, microphone in hand, I launched into one of my best-ever renditions of the "Star-Spangled Banner." I later told people that the 10,000 meters had opened my lungs.

Then it was time for the next event: the mile. I was registered for this one as well, and a mere 30 minutes after my 10,000, I was back on the starting line. Then, later in the day, came the 3,000.

In the mile, I ran 6:27. It was a single-age record for 76-year-olds, though well shy of the 75–79 age-group mark. So too with the 3,000, which I ran in 12:22: three records in one day. If it was hockey, I could call it a hat trick!

## MGM Aftermath: London—1955

In the control offices of Abbey Road's studios, John, Wilfred, and I listened to playbacks of the various takes of my two songs. Over a light supper, we discussed them. Everyone thought we had a winner, and even I, often my own worst critic, was pleased, although I thought I could have done better with the high notes at the end of "Mardi Gras." Still, the end product was quite good, and the songs made a nice pair.

"There Was a Time" was slower, more dramatic. "Mardi Gras" was robust, upbeat.

Then came the waiting, luckily not more than a couple of weeks.

The record was an old-style 45 rpm vinyl, with one song on each side, and was about the diameter of a tea saucer. It bore a yellow label asserting that it was by MGM, and there on the label was my name, even if it was Keston, rather than Caston. Yellow had always been my favorite color, so it seemed a particularly good omen.

It was a culmination of a years-old dream, the singer's equivalent of a runner winning a major race and comparable to the sense of triumph I felt when I finally broke 40:00 for 10K and proved myself worthy to challenge Alex Ratelle. In their respective arenas, both were among the high points of my life.

• • •

The next step was to promote the record. I sang in youth clubs, workingmen's clubs, and for the armed forces—anywhere John could book me. None could pay, but the goal was promotion. If it succeeded, I would be a star and money would not be a problem.

Weeks passed and the record sold steadily. It refused to break into the big time, but stardom remained tantalizingly close. The BBC started playing both songs on the radio, on call-in shows with names like *Housewives' Choice* and *Family Favorites*. I recruited every woman I knew to request them: my mother, my sisters, aunts, nieces, cousins, relatives near and distant, friends from the theater—anyone who might masquerade as a housewife making a choice. Each called in several times a week to ask for John Keston's rendition of "Mardi Gras" or "There Was a Time." They used different names each time, but they clearly weren't the only ones making the request because the songs continued to do well.

But still, record sales refused to really take off, so John suggested I start singing on the BBC's live programs. Since that was another long-term dream, I was happy to let him act as my agent. He contacted several BBC directors but always received the same response: I needed to go through the normal channels, via a formal request for an audition. That meant filling out an application form and then waiting until the music-program board of directors got around to reviewing it. With the BBC already playing two of my songs, it was infuriatingly slow. I had applied before, on my own, and it had taken months for them to review the application (turning me down, of course).

Now they were quicker but again rejected me. John went to bat for me—again—arguing that I wasn't simply a wannabe, I was a legitimate performer, possibly an up-and-coming star. This time, they listened to him, and I had my audition.

I should have gone into the audition full of confidence and anticipating a good result. After all, the BBC was playing my songs. But the impostor syndrome was again undermining my confidence. At Abbey Road, I had been in the zone. Now, I was shaking, suffering palpitations, and generally so nervous that I knew my first notes weren't up to snuff.

Sometimes, when this happened, I would begin to settle down after the first few bars. Hearing myself then producing reasonably decent sounds, despite the nerves, I would gain confidence. But you cannot run a world record 10K—or marathon—if you severely muff the first mile. I was cordially dismissed and told I would be notified in a week or so.

Two weeks later, I received a form letter from the director. "After reviewing your audition tape," it said, "the auditioning committee and I have found your voice to be unsuitable for broadcasting."

It was a staggering blow. Had it said: "We found you too nervous for live performance," I might have understood. But here was yet another person telling me I did not have the voice for my chosen profession. Part of me wanted to crawl in a hole and die. Another wanted to point out that my songs were still being played on their radio, so what the heck was wrong with my voice?

# CHAPTER 8

# Cable Street Blackshirt

## London—1995

According to the age-grading tables, I would lose about two minutes of marathon speed between my 70th and 71st birthdays. That translates to one second every three days, which doesn't sound like much but adds up rather quickly. Obviously, it's not that precise; you have good races and bad ones, but each day the clock continued to tick and my goal became incrementally more difficult. Time mattered, and I wanted to waste as little of it as possible before making another attempt.

Twice now, events beyond my control had robbed me of my goal. Surely it wouldn't happen again.

I waited two months this time, picking the London Marathon as my target. It's a flat, scenic course that had already seen some screamingly fast times, and it was a perfect course for my own goal. I still felt fit and ready and had learned important lessons about food and hydration. No way was I going to compromise my hard-earned fitness by eating bad food or not drinking enough along the way.

The race was also an opportunity to renew my acquaintance with old friends and favorite haunts. I spent two weeks in the Cotswolds, doing what runners call "tapering"—which is the gradual reduction in training that precedes a hard race. Properly done, it can be just as important as the training that precedes it. I ran easily on country lanes, pathways, and the ruins of the old Roman road from London to Bath. The ancient Roman cobbles were grass covered, affording a soft, gentle surface that was a nice antidote to the asphalt and concrete I had seen too much of in prior months. Even though I was tapering, I could run 10 or 11 miles without overtaxing myself on this road. A rime of frost sometimes covered the grass, the April air was bracing, and the songs of skylarks made me wish the race was now!

Two days before the big day, a friend named Max Jones took charge of me and insisted that I join him at his son's home, somewhat nearer to the starting line. Unlike most of my running friends, Max is nearly my age, and I had known him for several years. A top-notch runner in his own right, Max would soon set a dozen world age-group records in ultramarathon events ranging from 30 miles to 24 hours. He had also run every London Marathon since its inception in 1981—one of only 40 people who could claim that honor. If I set the record here, he would be nearly as thrilled as if he had done it himself. I could beat Max by several minutes, but my instructions from him were simple: hold back and don't run away from him before mile three.

The race was on Sunday. On Saturday, we went for an easy walk, then to a soccer match. It's a game that prizes both quickness and endurance, and watching the players, I concluded that they might make good marathoners. In a typical match, a well-conditioned forward will run upward of six miles in a constant start-and-stop manner that is very much like a runner's interval training. Maybe an entire generation of middle-aging soccer players will someday join the ranks of masters runners when their bodies tire of their game's many collisions.

After a substantial supper—the marathoner's carboloading delight—Max and I made final preparations for the big day. We pinned our race numbers to our shirts, packed a change of clothing to be shipped to the finish, and checked again to make sure our water bottles were full for the drive to London. No dehydration this time! I would start drinking before dawn and continue throughout the race!

Midnight came and went before we finished, but that was no problem. Life in the theater had made me a night owl, and I had long ago discovered that it isn't the lack of sleep on the night before the race that matters—it's making sure you were well rested the night before that. When singing, I had concluded that going light on sleep the night before an important morning event might be a benefit. Otherwise, it took forever to warm up my voice, and the result never felt good. The same seemed to apply to races. Perhaps it's because your core temperature drops as you sleep, and the longer you sleep, the longer it takes to bring it back to normal. All I know is that just as it was easier to warm up for singing on limited sleep, so too was it easier to warm up for a race.

By 5 A.M., I was awake. Max and I drank tea—strong, with milk and sugar (how else?)—and breakfasted on PowerBars. We drove to Charing Cross railway station and then boarded a train to the race start, in the London suburb of Blackheath.

With thirty thousand runners scheduled to participate, Charing Cross was a madhouse. On the train, I eavesdropped on the chatter of marathoners: stories of triumphs past, tips about races that were well organized and ones that were not, and worries about this or that nagging pain. I myself had no such concerns. I was in tip-top shape, more than good enough for what I needed. Today would be the day!

The start was divided into three sections, lining up on separate streets and not converging until a couple of miles into the race. Mine, the smallest of the three, included everyone over age 60 plus about five thousand of the faster men. It was chilly—only 38 degrees—but I knew it would warm up. Besides, I had lived 16 years in Minnesota. I knew how to run in the cold.

Staying warm at the start, though, was a different matter. The only facilities were tents. The men had one, the women another. In the tent, I began stretching, thinking how wonderful it would be to run the world record here on my native soil, in the town where I was born.

Technically, if I got the record, it would be a British national record as well. Some years ago, I had applied for U.S. citizenship, in part because I was posting times that would have been U.S. records had I only been a citizen. Ironically, I would now be a citizen were I not running this race. I had postponed my swearing-in because I would be here on the originally scheduled date.

Waiting for the start was making me nervous. Not only did I know how much it would mean for Max if I succeeded, but my quest had received enough coverage in the London papers that it now felt like opening night in the theater.

Nerves are a great diuretic. So too is cold air. All of it was compounded by an aging prostate and my determination that this time, I would not dehydrate. Add in the fact that I was in a tent full of other seniors in the same predicament, and there simply weren't enough toilets. Not far away, though, was a dense growth of bracken with dozens of bushes, all being frequented by racers making last-minute comfort calls. In the United States, this might have inspired jokes, but decorum is ingrained into us British, and nobody gave even the tiniest hint that he acknowledged what the others were doing.

In the tent, I hunched up my knees, trying to stay warm, sitting on a plastic bag (the grass was more than damp) gleaned from some kind soul who had come better prepared than I. With each passing moment, I felt less like the elite septuagenarian runner that the prerace publicity had dubbed me. Left to my own devices, I would have staved off the nerves by not coming to the start so early, but the need to take the subway and make sure we weren't late had mandated an absurdly early arrival. With nothing useful to do but sit on the plastic bag, there was no way to ward off worries. Had I carboloaded properly? Was there something else I should have done? Why hadn't I brought a throwaway sweatshirt so I could at least stop shivering? Why was I here, two and one-half hours before the start? Why wasn't I back in bed?

The time dragged. The race didn't start until 9 A.M., and everything had gone so efficiently leaving with Max that we had gotten here in a mere 90 minutes. Now I would have appreciated a bit of a traffic jam. Then I would merely have been nervous about missing the start!

I talked to other runners. Listened half-heartedly to the banter of those who had run this race before. Smelled the scents of a half-dozen liniments. Should I be rubbing something on myself? And still it was an hour and 10 minutes before the start. What else could I do? Maybe I should pee again. "You lose a minute a mile for every pound you are overweight," Max had instilled into my now slightly addled brain. No, that couldn't be right. That would mean that if I lost seven pounds, I would finish before I started. Maybe it was a minute throughout the entire race. What was my proper weight, anyway? It didn't matter. If I peed out another ounce, I would be that much faster, and it was something to do, and besides, the potty line had lessened enough that I no longer had to resort to the bushes.

I had never before encountered a race like this, which just wouldn't start—where there was nothing to do, for hours and hours. Finally, it was time to do a true warm-up, jogging gently so as not to burn off too much energy and stopping several times to stretch. I frittered away the final 40 minutes this way, gradually becoming reenergized and optimistic. May I never again have to go to a start so early! But now I really was ready. *Ready, ready, ready*, I told myself, going back into the tent one last time. I was no longer shivering. I was actually willing to talk to my fellow athletes—aware that there was more to running than records, that what it was really about was maintaining our fitness and our respect for ourselves. Listening to other seniors share their accomplishments and goals on this brisk British morning made me proud to be one of these dedicated and dynamic gentlemen. If I could break the record here, I would be doing it not just for myself, but for all of us. That wasn't pressure: it was motivation! Above all, it is my life's quest to persuade others to exercise daily for health, wellness, and sanity—and above all, to recognize who we are and what we can accomplish with commitment and application.

I had come full circle. I was finally, again, ready to race.

•  •  •

Max had been with me as I went through my prewarm-up hell, but I don't remember what, if anything, he said or did. Now he took charge of me again. "Don't go out too fast," he said for the hundredth time. "Stay with me. I'll keep you on pace." The weather was blossoming into a fresh, sunny morning, and as the cold fled, I could feel the optimism renewing me.

Then the gun sounded and off we went. Max tapped my arm and reminded me to stay with him. My target pace was 6:53, but I was to start 10 seconds per mile slower.

At first, even that pace was difficult among the melee of bodies. But when the press starts to abate and you finally find running room, you tend to overcompensate. Instead of holding with Max for three miles, I started to pull away after three-quarters of a mile. I tried to slow, but the younger fellows around me (all in at least their 40s or 50s) made that difficult, and I was drawn with them by the need to protect my space and not get kicked from behind.

The first mile went by at 6:54. That was faster than planned, but with Max lost in the crowd, I was now running the race my way, not his. That meant getting a little bit of time in the bank in the first part, as a hedge against the inevitable slowdown. I was one second behind target pace, which was good, but not good enough. Feeling strong and confident, I stepped up my pace for the second mile. And while Max might not be with me where I could hear his warnings, his recommendations persisted in my subconscious: "Be careful; don't go out too fast." I had run a lot of marathons. Max was right, but his plan had been too conservative, and my body had known it; that's why it had rebelled. A 6:54 start was perfect. Now, I ran a 6:44. *Good,* I thought, *a cushion for the later stages*! Mile three was similar, and I was feeling comfortable. This part of the course was slightly downhill and *should* be fast. Now I was passing younger runners who had gone out too fast and were already faltering, but I wasn't running too fast because I had been training at this pace ever since Valencia. Mile four went by at about the same pace, and I was into what I can describe only as a beautiful rhythm, feeling no effort and cruising among the young folk, exchanging occasional compliments and "Good day"s.

"'Ere, 'ow old are you, Dad?" one young fellow asked as I moved by. When I told him, he called to everyone within earshot: "D'you 'ear that, you blokes, Dad's 70 years old and he's leavin' us in the dust."

I told him about my goal. "Cor blimey, it's bloody marvelous, mate; I 'ope I can be jus' runnin' when I'm your age. Wot is the record tha' ya' tryin' for?"

I told him I had to break 3:01:14 for the record but that I wanted to go under three hours. "Cor, three hours 'e's 'opin' for, you blokes," he called out again. "'Ow about three 'earty cheers to 'elp 'im on 'is way. 'Ip 'ip 'ooray!" he prompted, and the chorus rang out around me three times.

It was elevating and pleasantly distracting.

"Let's keep up wiv 'im an' 'elp 'im get 'is record," my cockney friend said to his mates, and for a while we ran 6:44s together. It was too fast for them, though, and eventually they bid me adieu.

Two easy miles had slipped by this way, and I was now at the Cutty Sark, a nineteenth-century tea clipper that held the record for the fastest voyage, fully laden, from Australia to London—certainly a good omen for my endeavor, if ever there was one! The three-masted sailing ship was built in 1869 and made the journey in 69 days. Now she sits on dry land, next to the Thames River, in the midst of a traffic circle.

Unfortunately, one of the other runners stopped to have his picture taken. I had drifted wide on the bend, trying to avoid congestion, so when he stopped in front of me and I charged into him, it was as much my fault as his. It cost me a double time penalty: a few seconds from the collision and a few more by not cutting the corner as I should have.

Mile nine brought the Surrey Docks. Only two of the original seven docks remain, and these have been converted to a recreational area with upscale "dockworker" pubs and restaurants. Having now lost my cockney cheering section, I was concentrating on running even splits. A 6:45 pace was still very comfortable, and at mile 10, I calculated that if I could sustain this pace for another 10 miles, I would have more than 2 1/2 minutes in the bank for the final six miles.

At mile 10, according to the race brochure, we would pass very close to the Mayflower Pub, where the Pilgrims had planned their voyage to the New

World. Most Americans would be surprised to discover that these early colonists, whom they view as so dour and grim, knew their way around a pint. They had planned to sail from here, but the mooring fees were too high and they shifted to Plymouth. I was reminded of my own emigration and soon-to-shift citizenship. In 15 years of running, I had never raced in England. I would never again do it as a Brit.

Mile 11 was another 6:45. Continuing at that pace brought me, a few minutes later, to Tower Bridge.

Tower Bridge is the bridge the citizens of the retirement community of Lake Havasu City, Arizona, allegedly thought they were buying when they purchased London Bridge, which had been scheduled for demolition in 1968. London Bridge is just a bridge. Tower Bridge is a drawbridge with tall, square towers. Its architecture compliments the Tower of London, close by, where political prisoners were once imprisoned, tortured, and beheaded. The drawbridge was built in 1894 and the original machinery, still in use, has never failed. There were plenty of symbols here for an aging runner.

As the course approached the bridge, then crossed it, we got our first distant views of the downtown skyline. Boats dotted the river, top-heavy with spectators, and the occasional sound of an air horn urged us onward. As the view widened, so did the road, and for the first time, there was plenty of running room.

We were now more than an hour into the race, and the day was appreciably warmer.

Shortly after the half-marathon mark, the course renarrowed, briefly choking down through a constricted segment of Cable Street. Inexplicably, the organizers had chosen this constricted zone for an aid station. Even here, far to the fore of the main pack, an enormous scrum was gathered around the water tables, impeding progress. A large sweaty hand landed on my shoulder and pushed me aside as some big bruiser dived for a drink. I was shoved so hard that I collided with another runner who was trying to get to the table. He tried to dodge clear, but that only made it worse. Our feet tangled and I went sprawling, skidding on the pavement.

I jumped up as quickly as I could, mesmerized by the sight of blood on my knee, elbow, and hip. It hurt, but that hardly mattered. Would it alter my stride?

Only three hundred meters away was Bloody Tower, one of the most infamous torture chambers in the Tower of London. I hadn't exactly been tortured, but if I had been looking for symbols, that would have been a bad one. So too was the fact that during my early childhood, Cable Street had been the scene of many fights between the Blackshirts (Britain's tiny Fascist Party) and the Socialists. The guy who had shoved me would have made a great Blackshirt.

The medics had seen my fall and pulled me, protesting, off the course. "Are you OK?" one asked. "Let me take a look at it. It'll only take a minute."

A minute was something I most emphatically did not want to waste, but it took nearly that long to convince them I was able to continue. Not only had I lost time arguing with the medics, but I had been jarred out of my rhythm and could feel that my pace had slowed.

Going into mile 13, the steady string of 6:45s had built up about a 90-second cushion. Now, at mile 14, I was only 40 seconds ahead of my three-hour target.

There are runners for whom a 40-second cushion would be enough. They somehow manage to speed up in the second half, a process referred to as "negative splitting" because the later mile split times are faster than the early ones. But it has never worked for me. My best races have all entailed minor slowdowns in the latter miles. If I don't accumulate a small cushion of time at the start, I'll slow down anyway and come up that much further shy of my goal.

About a quarter of a mile back onto the course, the pinched-down section of Cable Street ended, and the course doubled in width. Why on earth hadn't they put the aid station here?

The next mile was a 6:50. I was still ahead of pace, but I desperately wanted back my lost 50 seconds. I was also still feeling shaky. But gradually, the sound of my feet comforted me, and I began slipping back into a more confident, economical running rhythm. I tried to concentrate on the "now" and not obsess about the fall. But it was difficult. I had never before fallen in a race. It just wasn't fair, especially when it was so clearly not my fault.

I continued clocking 6:50s through mile 18. Still less than a minute in the bank, but at least I was still putting it in, rather than taking it out. Meanwhile, the London landmarks continued to roll by. Particularly notable was the eight hundred-foot office tower at the center of Canary Wharf. No longer a dockyard, the wharf has matured into one of the largest business districts in the world, and its centerpiece tower cast a long shadow across the course. As we moved out of the sun, I realized that the temperature had been rising rapidly.

"I wish we could stay in the shade the rest of the way," a voice beside me said, and I concurred. April in London is not supposed to be hot, and I had not considered heat when preparing for this race. Nor had the weather report been cause for concern: it had called for a high of 60 degrees, and even that shouldn't have come until long after I was finished. Now, it was at least 70 degrees and rising. By the end of the race, it would hit 78 degrees, only two degrees shy of the temperature that had parched me in Valencia. But this time, at least I was getting water whenever I wanted it. I was also taking the sports drink—the same Isostar I had spurned in Valencia. Prior to the race, I had tried it in training and found no quarrel between it and my stomach.

Soon we were back in the sun. I still had plenty of energy, and my scrapes no longer hurt, but from mile 18 to 19, my pace fell to 6:57. Even if you're well hydrated, heat takes a toll, and I was now beginning to withdraw seconds from the "time bank." Had I saved up enough?

Mile 20 was worse, but not badly so: 6:58. However this came out, it was going to be very close. The course was wide, the pack had thinned, and my space was safe. I was no longer at risk of being pushed, cut off, bumped, or stepped on. A few runners were now passing me, but I was passing even more. All were far younger.

It was getting hotter by the mile. The warmth from the dark pavement invaded my shoes and made my feet burn. Ahead, the air shimmered. Shadows were rare. I was no longer paying attention to landmarks. At mile 21, I threw a cupful of water over myself and did my sums for the umpteenth time. I had clocked a 7:10, which meant I still had nearly 30 seconds in the bank. But 7:10s weren't going to cut the mustard. Damn that fall! Blast that man who had so rudely shoved me, and blast the race directors for creating such a mess in the first place. Back in middle of the pack, that aid station must be bringing the race to an utter standstill.

It was all so frustrating that I wanted to scream, but marathon running is, above all, about discipline. I did my best to pick up the pace.

Somewhere between miles 22 and 23, the course circles back past another side of the Tower of London, running on cobblestones for about four hundred meters, past the Traitors' Gate. Three or four yeoman warders stood at attention, their splendid uniforms dotting the course with color. Also adding color was a blue carpet laid out to provide easier footing across the cobbles. Unfortunately, it was only 2 meters wide. There wasn't room for everyone, and I noticed that some runners were bypassing it even when they didn't need to. I found out why when I tripped on a rucked-up section and nearly fell again.

Now we were in the old City of London, passing the Billingsgate Fish Market, where fish once was stored on ice. Even though the market hadn't been used for decades, the race brochure said that centuries of cold storage had created so much permafrost under the building that it was once 3 feet thick.

I again tried to rally, but by mile 24 I knew I was badly off pace. I had given up paying attention to my watch, but I was still pushing the button to save the times at each mile marker. I later discovered I had run a 7:20, which was about what it felt like. My three-hour dream was gone. The world record was 74 seconds slower. It was still in reach. Breaking it by a single second would be fine.

Parliament Square and Big Ben came into view as I pushed harder, trying for that last iota of speed. As we hit the last straightaway before the finish on the Mall, just past Buckingham Palace, crowds lined the street six or seven deep. Somewhere among them were my friends and family, but I never heard their voices, so focused was I on trying to go just that last tiny bit faster.

Shortly after mile 24, a young fellow in his upper twenties had caught me, but instead of passing and pushing ahead for his own best-possible finish, he stayed with me, doing his best to pace me to whatever might be the best time we could accomplish together. I told him what I needed: anything better than 3:01:14. He knew that if we could just pick up the pace enough on the final mile, we could do it. I ran hard through mile 26, past the palace and onto the Mall . . . and there was the clock, ticking my fate away. 3:01:10, 3:01:11, 3:01:12 . . .

I finished in 3:01:35, knowing that but for the fall I would have had it with time to spare. If the weather had just been cool, as it was supposed to be, I might have had it anyway. If, if, if. Three races and three enormous ifs. I wasn't a runner, I was a walking jinx. There was a consolation prize: I had set a British national record and broken the course record for my age group, smashing it so thoroughly that as far as I know, it still stands.

The medics at the finish line had apparently heard about my fall and my refusal of medical attention because they were waiting for me when I went to the medical tent in search of treatment. "You're unbelievably fit," said the young doctor who treated me, offering up another consolation prize. "I wish I could just run a marathon, let alone do it in nearly three hours."

Still, I was deeply disappointed, and the old stubbornness was rearing its head. I should have done better. I *could* do better. I *would* do better.

I didn't know where my next attempt would be, but I did know there would be one, and it would be soon because I wasn't getting any younger. Besides, summer was looming, and cool, fast courses would soon be in short supply.

Meanwhile, what I wanted was a pint of good English bitter. I found Max, who had run 3:20:17, rounded up my sweats, and waded through the throng in search of my cheering squad. As soon as I found them, we hit the nearest pub for a couple of good 'uns and steak and kidney pie. All the while, my subconscious was churning through prospects for my next race.

John as Olympic torchbearer in Independence, Oregon, 1986.

John finishing the London Marathon, 22 seconds short of a new world record for the 70–75 age group, but getting the course record this day in April 1995.

John is airborne during a training run.

John and son Tony in the 1997 Turin Marathon. They started 30 minutes before the open elite. John was trying to break his own 70–74 world record of 3:00:58 by going under 3 hours.

John with a police escort in the 1997 Turin Marathon.

John at age 68 finishing the Pear Blossom 10-miler in 63:08 (6:18 pace), setting the course record for 65–69.

John as Gehn in the famous computer game *Riven*.

John as Vittorio Vidal, an Italian film star, in a scene from the musical *Sweet Charity* with Juliette Prowse.

John (center) as King Nikki in Ivor Novello's
musical, *King's Rhapsody.*

John playing Alfred Steiglitz
in a PBS documentary.

John (left) as Sherlock Holmes in a Brooke Bond Tea commercial.

John (right) in a Kit Kat sailing commercial in the United Kingdom before the candy was introduced to the American market.

John and his wife, Anne, after the 1997 Portland Marathon.

Greater trochanter repair in 1997. John set more world and American records after this surgery than before.

John singing the national anthem before the 2007 Lilac Bloomsday 12K in Spokane, Washington.

## CHAPTER 9

# Something to Prove

### Alvo Berti: London—1955

The BBC was still playing my songs, and for a while, it seemed I might yet make the big time. But ultimately, stardom eluded me. The record sold thirty thousand copies—a nice number in today's CD-driven world but a drop in the bucket in the days of vinyl, when production costs were higher. Once again, I was on Gigli's doorstep: on the verge of my dream but defeated by the final step.

My money began to run low, and Mariolina couldn't take a job because she was too busy with the boys. To avoid the ignominy of being on the dole, I took a job in a department store. That led to an offer from Phillips Electrical Company—the very company whose record label I had been planning to audition for when John Michelson intercepted me for MGM. But the job had nothing to do with music. Phillips is a large company, and I wound up as a sales promoter for electric shavers, the brand known in the United States as Norelco. It was the most prestigious day job I had ever held, and the company gave me a car and sent me on road trips, where I set up demonstrations at county fairs and worked to boost the business of wholesalers and store managers. It was a good product and I was a good salesman. Mariolina was proud, the company was pleased, my customers were happy. Basically, everyone thought that if I couldn't be a recording star, this was a lot better than being a starving actor.

But I was already plotting my next assault on show business. What I needed was a way to get over the fear that crippled me in auditions. What I needed was to put my self-doubts behind me. Besides, I had something to prove to the folks at the BBC who had happily played my song, all the while telling me I couldn't sing.

What I needed was to be someone else.

His name was Alvo Berti, and I created him during those long road trips for Phillips. It would take nerve to pull it off—nerve and gall. Not exactly my strong suits, but Alvo was a character, not me, and what I needed to do was to view him in that manner. He would be suave and self-assured and everything I wasn't. He would prove something to me as well as to the BBC.

At home, Mariolina and I spoke nothing but Italian. I had even perfected the dialect of her hometown, Casale Monferrato in Piemonte. Now, after work, I spent every spare moment preparing a new repertoire of arias and Neapolitan folk songs.

Several months later, when enough time had passed for most of the people at the BBC to have forgotten John Keston, I wrote again to the auditions department, informing them that I, Alvo Berti, was a professional opera singer, recently come to England. In order to avoid being assigned the same pianist I had gotten in my John Keston audition—the person most likely to see through my guise—I let Alvo add "dat I wood be bringing my oun piano plaier."

Today, someone at the BBC would have phoned or e-mailed somebody in Italy, and the ruse would have collapsed. In the 1950s, international communication was more difficult. Nobody checked my references, and in due course, Alvo was invited to audition.

Now the worries began. Just as, years later, I would find myself at the start of the London Marathon with nothing to do but fret and shiver, I had five weeks with nothing to do but watch the slow circuit of the hours. I wasn't so much worried about performing well—my new character Alvo could handle those worries quite well—it was my fear that someone would catch me. My mind kept playing over those horrible moments in the mid-Atlantic, when my commanding officer had summoned me to his office and told me that I had been found out, that I was too young to be in the RAF. Only this time, as when I had turned myself in for desertion, there would be no "thanks for being so patriotic" reprieve. There would merely be humiliation.

I suppose Alvo could have suffered a family emergency and escaped back to Italy. But I never seriously entertained the thought of giving up, just as later, I would never voluntarily give up in a race. I might be beaten, but I wouldn't quit.

And there really wasn't much that could trip me up, other than an unfortunate meeting with someone who knew me as John Keston. Even if there were Italians on the audition panel, they would never catch on. Nor would anyone know I wasn't the "real" Alvo Berti because it was a totally fictitious name and I had been careful to avoid giving him a resume that would make them think they should have heard of him. He was good, but not *that* good.

I had invented the name because it sounded so wondrously Italian. The florid, open vowels, the rolled *r*, and the hard consonants glided easily over my tongue. Both names ended with lovely open sounds. It was, as John Michelson had desired for my English name, "euphonious." If it didn't actually exist in Italian, it certainly should have.

I practiced saying it, over and over. "Aaahlvoo Berrteee." I let myself become so Italian that surely my alter ego would convince even an Italian judge, especially because I would be speaking in front of my audition panel in the distinctive Piemonte dialect. It was just a role, I told myself for the thousandth time, just a role.

To help stay in character, I bought a new wardrobe. Now, dressed to the nines—or should I say *nove?*—in crumpled linen trousers, matching silk shirt, silk cravat, cashmere waistcoat, yellow socks, and light-brown, brushed-suede shoes, I thoroughly looked the part. I even got an Italian leather briefcase for my music.

Although Mariolina wasn't thrilled with my return to theater—she liked the financial security of my job with Phillips—she agreed to accompany me to the audition. Along with my accompanist—an old friend who was in on the joke—we arrived at the BBC and were ushered to the studio where the audition would take place. Keeping up the façade, I talked loudly with Mariolina in the Piemonte dialect. Then I turned to the BBC assistant who was leading me to the audition room. "Cooda I warrm uppa my voicea?"

I didn't need it—my accompanist and I had practiced for an hour at another studio—but it was something Alvo would expect. The assistant gave me 10 minutes. While I was putting Alvo through his paces, the auditioning director asked me to give the technicians a voice level. Would I sing the loudest and highest passage from any of my audition pieces, please? He was the same director who had auditioned John Keston several months earlier, and my heart nearly stopped.

To hide my shock, I turned to Mariolina. *Che pensi, devo praticarmi un pezzo di Tosca?* "Should I practice a little of the *Tosca?*" I was frantically trying to stay in character, and conversing with her in Italian, just as though we were at home, helped settle me so I wouldn't blow either my cover or Alvo's audition.

I needn't have worried. The director was charmed. He asked where in Italy I was from, and I told him that "I wassa from Casale Monferrato nee'er Torino." Mariolina's hometown. To the question of where I had trained, I truthfully answered that I had studied with Alfredo Morelli, presidente of the Conservatorio di San Pietro a Majella in Napoli.

My primary audition piece was the aria "E Lucevan le Stelle" from Puccini's *Tosca*. Confidence returning, I gave the engineer his recording level and the audition proceeded. I sang a total of two arias and two Neapolitan folk songs. I was in fine voice and was feeling that I had acquitted myself well when the director called down from the recording booth and asked whether I had any English songs in my repertoire. I hadn't anticipated that, but I told him in my best Italian accent that "I cooda singa 'Ooh Dahnee Boyee,' da Irissha songa." In the not too distant past I had heard a recording of the great Caruso singing that sad Irish classic, so, emulating his accent, I performed it with the best Latin emotion I could muster.

Then the audition was over, and I was again told I would be notified by mail within a fortnight. Singing and the nervous energy of staying in character had worked up an appetite, so throwing Alvo to the wind, but still wearing his fancy clothes, I took Mariolina to the nearest fish and chips shop to have a thoroughly English meal. If anyone from the studio had spotted me, I would have told them that Alvo *volevo provare mangiare Inglese*—meaning that he "wanna try eata like Eenglish."

## Flat and Fast: Kelowna, British Columbia—1995

Back in the United States, I pored over ads in running magazines, looking for a course where, barring food poisoning, torrid temperatures, or large, aggressive competitors, I might actually run the race I knew was possible. Within days, I found one in the *National Masters News*, the publication whose tip, a few months earlier, had sent me to Valencia.

It was the inaugural Okanagan Marathon in Kelowna, a town of about one hundred thousand in south-central British Columbia.

It would be the fourth country in which I had raced in as many attempts, but British Columbia was just up the road from Oregon. I wouldn't need to fly, and it seemed far enough north to make heat an unlikely risk, at least in May. So I called up the director and asked about the course.

Oh yes, he said. It's flat and very fast. "Definitely a PR course." I told him what I wanted to do, and he became increasingly enthusiastic. What a coup it would be if a world record was run on the course its first year. If I would make the attempt, the race would pay for my hotel.

A flat, scenic course was exactly what I wanted, and I accepted immediately. Start-up events can have their drawbacks, but the director was manager of the local Running Room store—a well-respected Canadian chain, noted for supporting good races and hosting training groups for athletes of all abilities. It should be a small but well-organized event, without the crowds that had been my undoing in London.

The drive was scenic and uneventful, and when I got to Kelowna, I discovered that the race director had researched my prior results and confirmed that I was who I said I was. If the BBC had been so thorough, Alvo Berti would never have gotten his audition. The local newspaper had been told of my presence, and copies of its articles were posted on the store walls, where they were read by other runners signing up at the last minute. Some even asked me for autographs. The excitement was infectious but lower key than at Valencia and not as intimidating. I found myself drawn into it, eager and ready to run.

The weather was fine and cool, and the Okanagan Valley deserved its reputation for beauty. Unlike coastal British Columbia, which is notorious for unremitting sogginess, the Okanagan is near desert, dry and sunny. In places, the natural vegetation is sagebrush, but a fledgling wine industry is making its presence felt, and if global warming continues, British Columbia may become the next great wine region.

I arrived Thursday night, two and a half days before the race. Normally, I like to spend the final days quietly: walking a little and running gently, doing a few fast strides or "pullouts" just to keep the legs from tightening up. But I was the celebrity of the moment, and the round of prerace meetings, newspaper interviews, and radio and TV appearances kept me too busy for my normal routine. Still, I was enjoying the hospitality of this charming town halfway between the Coast Range and the Rockies.

Then the race director gave me a private tour of the course. I didn't want to go—I really do have a superstitious fear that seeing a course ahead of time would somehow curse me—but there was no way to decline graciously.

On the phone from Oregon, he had explained that the race, the first marathon ever held in the Okanagan Valley, would start in town, which lay on the shores of Lake Okanagan, which threads for miles through its namesake valley. It would head out into the country for a dogleg to another lakeshore vantage point, then return to town, visiting new neighborhoods en route to a Valencia-style finish on the high school track.

With the benefit of hindsight, a red flag was buried in that simple description. If you start on a lake, move inland, and then return to the lake, you have to cross some sort of headland. That meant there had to be at least a bit of a hill each way on that out-and-back dogleg.

The moment I saw it, I knew I was in trouble. All runners know that "perfectly flat" courses usually aren't. Partly it's the near-universal tendency of race directors to exaggerate, but there is also the problem that "flat" is a relative term. I suppose the folk of Kelowna, sandwiched between seven-thousand-foot mountain ranges, can be forgiven if their use of the term overlooks a few minor inclines. But this "perfectly flat" course was considerably hillier than I had been led to believe.

Everyone I had met here was kind, gracious, and charming. But there was no hiding one critical fact: when it came to the course description, I had been had. Much of the course was indeed flat, but that headland entailed a sharp climb followed by a very long drop to the lake. Then I would have to turn around, slog back up, and come pounding back down.

Still, I wasn't used to previewing courses from a car. Maybe the hills weren't as bad as they looked.

• • •

With that attitude, I slept well and awoke rested and eager to run. I presented myself at the start with plenty of time to warm up but not having to sit around for hours, as I had done in London. I jogged a bit to get the blood circulating, stretched, and then took my place at the front of the pack with the young elites. My plan was simple: start at 6:45s and see what happened. I knew I could hold that pace for at least 16 miles. If I slowed to 6:50s in the next four, then dropped to 7:00s for the final miles, I would make it.

I also knew I would lose some time in the hills, so I was slightly ahead of pace when I hit the first one. The climb slowed me, and then the long descent started at mile seven. I let the downgrade pull me forward, trying to get back on target pace. Runners were now coming toward me from the turnaround, and I was startled by how few there were; I was quite far up in the pack.

The lake was a gorgeous blue, speckled with sailboats, downtown Kelowna shimmering on the far side. It truly was a spectacular setting. But I had lost more time than I liked on the ascent and hadn't made all of it up on the drop. Turning around and going back up the hill sucked more time out of me, and now I was being passed by younger runners who were better hill runners than I or had done a better job of pacing the first bounce. They had all read about me, and they waved encouragement as I slogged up that endless rise.

The rest of the race was uneventful, going through charming residential neighborhoods, all basically flat. I maintained a nice, steady pace through mile 23 but never made back the time I had lost on the hills. It was also warming up, heading (again!) for the 70s. With three miles to go, I was about a minute off my world-record target, en route to something on the order of a 3:02:15 if I didn't lose more time. The increasing heat slowed me a bit more, and I eventually settled for 3:02:51.

Afterward, the race officials continued to treat me like royalty, and a local grocery store presented all of the finishers with one of the finest postrace spreads I had ever seen. That evening, at a party in one of the race officials' homes, out on that beautiful lakeshore, I was again feted and invited to come back next year.

I told them I would think about it. It really was a well-run event, but I had again been defeated by things that had nothing to do with my training. Not only were the hills a factor, but Kelowna lies at an elevation of 1,400 feet. That didn't seem all that high to me at the time, but I've subsequently learned that even a modest elevation can slow you down: in the case of 1,400 feet, only by about 1 percent, but I was closer than that to my target. Despite the heat and hills, an equivalent effort at sea level might have netted it.

At the time, though, I knew only that the defeat was my own fault. I should have taken a pass on Kelowna and looked for something flatter.

## Change of Plans: London—1955

Alvo Berti did not receive a sorry-but-your-voice-is-unsuitable letter. Instead, he was informed that he had passed the preliminary audition. Presuming he passed a final audition that now needed to be scheduled, he would be called in for live performances of material to be chosen for him at a later date by the BBC's directors. Apparently, my voice was indeed suitable for broadcasting.

It was the greatest "So there!" of my performing career, comparable to the one I later scored with Twin Cities Marathon director Jack Moran, when I ran that 39:24 in the Freeze Y'r Gizzard Blizzard Run, though at least in the race I did it under my own name.

I went in for the final audition not caring about the outcome. Not caring, I had no trouble singing well—a different set of songs, all Italian. This time, I was effusively complimented by the audition director, who told me he was sure the BBC would soon be calling me to perform.

It is possible that I could have made a career as Alvo Berti. The main problem would have been that the accountants would have needed to know my true name in order to pay me without committing tax fraud. That would have tipped off the music directors, who might not have wanted to take the risk of foisting off a fake Italian tenor on the British public. Singing under a stage name is never truly fraud, but neither was the Alvo Berti deception the same type of thing as changing from Caston to Keston. With Alvo, I had created an entirely fictitious personality to go with the name, and that's best done as an open joke, the way Peter Schickele later did on American public radio with a "lost" member of the Bach family, P. D. Q. Bach.

Nor did I want to play the part of Alvo forever. So after the director finished praising me, I switched to my most cultured theatrical English and thanked him. Then, figuring I was burning my bridges with the BBC once and for all, I told him I was John Keston, whose voice he had twice before found unsuitable.

I shudder to think of how that revelation might have been greeted today, but in the 1950s, we British prided ourselves on graciousness. The audition director blinked nicely, recovered his poise, and averred that I had not only played a splendid joke on his organization but also made my point. He even went so far as to promise that the deception would not be held against me and that John Keston might well get the call to perform in lieu of Alvo Berti—it being, after all, the same voice and the same music.

I was surprised. I had expected to be shown the door—politely, but firmly. Nevertheless, I asked him to drop me from the BBC's list of singers. Driving the English countryside with my electric shavers, I had had plenty of time for thinking, and not all of it was about Alvo Berti and the BBC. I had decided it was time to emigrate. As soon as possible, I was moving to Canada.

## CHAPTER 10

# The New World

### *At Sea Again: Mid-Atlantic Ocean—1955*

The decision to leave England wasn't made on impulse; at least three factors contributed to it. One was the postwar economy, which wasn't bright. Another was that Mariolina and I weren't doing well. She had cheered for my record and lent her energy to the Alvo Berti deception, but my dreams were not hers, and hers were not mine. She would have been happy to see me climb the corporate ladder at Phillips; I never saw that as anything but a way station from which to recoup some cash and plan my next assault on the stage.

Also, Alvo Berti had taught me I could accomplish much by starting anew. I had the talent, but in the background always lurked the schoolboy not good enough for the chorus. Alvo had been free of him and in his brief fictitious career had achieved something that had eluded me for years: the ability to present himself well in audition. There had been nerves, for sure—as there would be years later when I was preparing for races—but they hadn't undercut me. That was a problem I wouldn't fully conquer until I developed a dual identity as an athlete and a performer, but Alvo helped point the way. He showed me something practical: he had scored a major coup with no true credentials but his voice.

And thus it was that I found myself once again aboard ship in the mid-Atlantic, not as a boy-soldier barely old enough to shave, but as an adult. Perhaps what had worked for Alvo could also work for me.

I chose Canada simply because I had relatives in Toronto and it was an easy emigration for a British citizen. But I truly hated to be so far from my sons. In those pre-jetliner days, North America was a long way away, and while I could send money back—more perhaps than I could make at home—I knew it might be a very long time before I could return to England. Mariolina and I, however, were clearly heading for a split, and in those days, joint custody was rare. Even if I stayed in England, I wouldn't be seeing a great deal of my sons. Nevertheless, it had been a very difficult decision.

• • •

The ship wasn't a troop carrier, but my accommodations weren't a lot better than before. But there was one wonderful bonus: the first-class section had a theater, and daytimes, I used it to practice.

Perhaps every musician has stories that begin with being overheard at practice. We have to practice a lot, and however discreet you try to be, it's necessary on occasions to be fairly loud. One day, an older couple stuck their heads in the door. Did I mind if they came inside and listened?

Each day for the rest of the weeklong voyage, they joined me. Between practice sessions, we swapped stories. They were opera lovers returning from vacation in Europe. They liked my voice, and they knew a theatrical agent who might be able to help me find work.

When the ship docked, we swapped addresses, then they went to their home in Denver while I moved on to Toronto. There, I fell back on my RAF skills to take a job with the De Havilland Aircraft Company, earning more money than I had with Phillips, sending regular checks back home and doing a job I enjoyed far more than demonstrating shavers. I also set to work doing what Alvo Berti had done: circulating my (real) resume to anyone looking for singers or actors.

One day, I received a letter from Denver.

I didn't need to read it to know who it was from—there were only two people in that city with any reason to write me. As I opened it, a hundred-dollar bill fell out.

In the 1950s, that was a lot of money—not quite equivalent to the one thousand dollars the Correcaminos club would later give me to race in Spain, but in the same ballpark. My friends were indeed well connected and wanted me to meet them in Chicago, where they thought they could get me a job. The money was for travel.

I couldn't go right away. My resume circulation had garnered several auditions and an appearance on a television variety show. I also had my job at De Havilland. But within two weeks, I got time off, and my friends booked me into the Conrad Hilton Hotel—a high-class establishment that would prove to be my home away from home for much of the following year.

The job they had found had come through a friend of their friend, who was an agent in Chicago. It was at an ice show that would be playing at the Conrad Hilton, in which skating numbers were choreographed around a storylike theme. I would do the male dialogue, a soprano would do the female dialogue, and we also got to sing. I landed it on the spot. It was a startling turn of events that I couldn't help but contrast to my return to London after the war, when my government wouldn't give a performing-arts grant to a soldier who had given five years of his life to his country. These near-strangers had done more for me in a few moments than my government, the BBC, or anyone but John Michelson and my Italian friends had done in a decade.

Today's ice shows are enormous spectacles like traveling circuses. They hold a small number of performances in enormous hockey arenas and then move on to the next city. This one was locally produced and would encamp at the Conrad Hilton for four months, performing two shows a night, seven days a week. It was small enough to be a dinner theater, with the ice laid out beneath the dance floor of the hotel's nightclub, which seated about three hundred people. At the start, the floor would roll back to reveal the ice. I would be on a small, nearby stage, wearing an absurd pink tuxedo with a rose-colored bowtie. I would take a lot of flak about this in months to come, but what mattered was that I had a contract for the run of the show—one that gave me room and board at the hotel plus enough money that I could accumulate some savings, even while still sending funds back to England.

Rehearsals started in five weeks, so I went back to Toronto to give notice at my aircraft job. Meanwhile, the producer set out to get me a work permit, something that required convincing Immigration that no American could do what I would be doing. When it concurred that I was more than just a generic singer, even the U.S. Immigration and Naturalization Service granted me greater recognition than I had ever received from my own government. It is one of many reasons why, as a U.S. citizen, I now seize any opportunity to sing "The Star-Spangled Banner" at the start of races.

• • •

The show was a success, and my friends came from Denver to see it. When the four months had run their course, the management decided there was an audience for a second show. A new one was written, and most of the original cast was retained, including me. My work permit was renewed, and while I was at it, I applied for a green card. Today those are hard to get, but in 1955, it was easy: I merely had to prove I wouldn't wind up on welfare by showing the INS that I had 1,200 dollars in cash. Thanks to the first show, I had it, and by the time the second show ended, I had the card.

I could now pursue any kind of work I wanted in the United States. That, of course, was a simple decision. There was only one type of work I had ever wanted to do.

• • •

Mariolina and I had been permanently parted now for nearly a year, and just as I was moving on with my musical life, I knew I also wanted a marriage that would stand the test of time. I didn't know I would find it by living on the hotel's 23rd floor.

Because my room was so high up, life involved a constant succession of elevator rides, and in the 1950s, elevators weren't the push-button affairs we know today: they required operators. One was a petite blonde in a pale blue uniform, with white gloves and blue eyes. She claims she was the one who made the first move, but I'm sure I noticed her long before she asked the bellman to introduce us.

Her name was Anne Norton. She had grown up in Oregon but was now doing masters work in classical speech and theater at Northwestern University.

Elevator operators got to sit on a little stool, and during slack times, she would study. One day, I noticed a book of Greek plays beneath her stool and asked about it. Soon it was obvious that we had three major interests in common: classical literature, Greece, and—most important—a love of oral interpretation in song, drama, and recitation. That gave us so much to talk about that neither of us ever felt awkward. More than 50 years later, we're still together.

• • •

In my spare time, I consulted a music arranger to develop a nightclub act that mixed popular music with show tunes, Neapolitan folk songs, and arias. My Chicago agent then booked me into a two-week engagement in a revue in a suburban club.

It wasn't the greatest production, with an undertrained chorus line prancing around like a cheap replica of Las Vegas. But the band was good and played my new arrangements quite nicely.

My next stop was an Italian restaurant in downtown Chicago where my native-sounding Italian and repertoire of Neapolitan songs were invaluable. One week, a rich Texan dined at the restaurant each night. He pronounced himself to be an opera lover, told me I was one of the finest tenors he had ever heard, and gave me a big tip every time I sang one of his requests. Typically it was 10 dollars per song—a staggering sum after all those years of poverty. On his last night, he tipped me 20 dollars, gave me his card, and told me to look him up if I was ever in his area. It was more of the New World at its most intriguing.

## Sheer Stupidity: McMinnville, Oregon—May 1995

Lawyers like to quip that any attorney who represents himself has a fool for a client. Self-coached runners suffer a bit of the same problem. It's not that you can't learn training theory from books, it's that you need the coach to tell you when you've gone off the deep end.

Following my experience in Kelowna, I had a full-blown case of an ailment I call *marathonitis*. It's similar to the condition that once caused me to try every young-man's workout I ever read about in *Runner's World*. Now it proved that, at least on occasion, age does not bring wisdom.

What I needed was to rest and regroup. But I had now been robbed of the world record four times, and in the last three races, I had missed it by a combined three minutes and 54 seconds. Averaged out over 78.6 miles, that was a mere three seconds per mile. The same arithmetic said I had missed breaking three hours by a mere six seconds per mile, despite conditions that seemed to have conspired against me each time.

One thing all those near misses had taught me was that the record was very much within reach. Another was that I needed to take charge and avoid unknowns. I figured it was time to run a course I knew.

Within days, I was scouring race listings, looking for the ideal one. Then I saw an announcement for the Clackamas River Canyon Marathon and knew the answer: I would return to the scene of my most recent sub-3:00. It had all the elements I needed: a fast, downhill course, cool weather, no crowds, and I could eat at home.

There was only one problem: it was a mere 13 days after Kelowna.

# Go West, Young Man: Chicago—1957

Anne was nearing the end of her graduate studies at Northwestern. Her roots were in Oregon, and now she invited me to come live on her parents' farm. "They can always use some help," she said, "and it's not far from Portland."

I was delighted by the idea. I had continued singing at the Italian restaurant, and while it was steady work, it wasn't challenging artistically. Staying with Anne was my top priority, but I was ready to try my hand at something else, and Oregon sounded like as good a place as any.

Oregon, however, was a long way away, and we needed to get there as inexpensively as possible. Airplanes were out of the question, buses were uncomfortable, and the rail would entail at least two nights of pricey Pullman cars. Then one morning, browsing the classified ads in the *Chicago Tribune*, I found one seeking a driver to take a car to Portland. I took the job, served notice to the restaurant, and began the depressingly easy job of packing—depressing because even between us, we had very few belongings to pack.

President Eisenhower had only recently authorized the interstate highway system, and today's freeways existed mostly in the dreams of engineers. That made the trip a five-day adventure on which I was completely captivated by the sprawling beauty of the American landscape. Except for a detour to Denver to visit my old friends, we followed the Lincoln Highway, better known as U.S. 30, which largely parallels the routes of Lewis and Clark and the Oregon Trail through the Midwest, Great Plains, Rocky Mountains, and Pacific Northwest.

I hadn't previously driven on the right-hand side of the road and was concerned that my attention would wander and I would veer into an oncoming truck. But Anne was a good copilot, reminding me that as long as I followed the traffic ahead of me, I wouldn't be tempted to wander to the British side of the road. Some parts of the road were lightly used, but others were heavily enough traveled that it was like following a vast pack of marathoners, all headed for the same destination.

Along the way, we stopped wherever we could while Anne regaled me with stories of the pioneers and whatever other tidbits of American history fit the parade of scenery.

Six days later, we had driven nearly two thousand miles—a distance that would have spanned an enormous chunk of Europe—dropped off the car, and taken up residence at the Nortons' farm, near the town of McMinnville. I was immediately made to feel welcome, both by the family and by the Willamette Valley terrain, which looked much like England. Even the trees were friendly. Horse chestnut, walnut, hazel, poplars, birch, maple, and oak make up much of the English country landscape, and seeing them here made the land familiar and inviting, while the distant, volcanic cone of 11,235-foot Mount Hood never let me forget I was in a new land.

My first concern was to find gainful employment. I located a couple of agents in Portland, but all they were able to find were minor engagements in nightclubs. They weren't enough, and nightclub performing wasn't my favorite work. Anne and I discussed it at length, and eventually, I decided to spend a few months in San Francisco. If that worked, she could join me later. For the moment, though, she had taken a school-teaching job in Oregon for at least a year. I didn't want to go on my own, but travel separations, sadly, would always be part of the life I had chosen.

## CHAPTER 11

# A Fine Oregon Rain

*E*stacada, Oregon—1995

No matter how fast I ran, I couldn't post an official world record at the Clackamas River Canyon Marathon. Even if I made my goal, it would merely be a "world's best."

There are rules for the type of course that can qualify for official world records, and the Clackamas course failed on two accounts. First, it was down-hill, and second, it was a point-to-point race where, in theory, you could be wind aided. For a course to qualify for a world record, it doesn't have to be a perfect loop, but the straight-line distance between start and finish can be no more than half the distance of the race: five kilometers for a 10K, ten kilometers for a 20K, and so forth.

A great many marathon courses fail to meet these requirements, but a world's best, set on a "good" course, can carry all the cachet of an official record. What matters is that the course is accurately measured, that you don't actually *have* a raging tail wind, and that you don't get too much of a gravity boost along the way.

By these standards, Clackamas was marginal. The course dropped nearly one thousand feet, and while it had some substantial upgrades, they by no means countered the advantage from the overall drop. Still, the course had been good enough a year ago to earn me the distinction of oldest man to go below three hours. If I could do it again, I could extend that honor to age 70 1/2. Even if I again missed my goal, it would be fun to run with my Oregon racing buddies and to reexperience that peaceful, rural course.

I wasn't really thinking clearly, but I think I believed it would be good karma. I thought I was still strong and getting stronger, and that even if the downhill course was a bit of cheat, setting a world's best on it would make me stronger yet for a subsequent attempt on a less dubious course.

My training strategy, such as it was, was to do very little running between the two marathons. In the first five days I ran a total of only 16 miles, partly because I had sustained serious blisters in Kelowna, and three days later they were still oozing blood. If I didn't let the blisters heal, nothing else mattered, anyway.

Much of what I did run was speed work, which now sounds insane. On Friday, five days after Kelowna, I ran several sets of 400s, 200s, and 100s at 83 seconds, 32 seconds, and 15 seconds, respectively. Then, on Saturday, I entered a track meet and won gold medals at 200, 800, and 3,000 meters, plus another as a member of a 4 × 400 relay team.

The following day, I decided to remind my body that I was a marathoner with an 11-mile run at a desultory pace on the logging trails near the home Anne and I had built in the mountains that form the western fringe of the Willamette Valley. I was feeling invincible, and the 11-miler seemed therapeutic at the time. But a coach, if I had had one, might have warned me that the moment you start feeling invincible, you're on the cusp of trouble. The next day I woke feeling sluggish enough that for the next two days, I needed to confine my activities to lawn mowing. A coach might also have informed me that sluggishness at this point was a bad sign, but instead I attacked it three days before the marathon with another session of 400s, 200s, and 100s on the track.

By race-day morning, it was obvious that heat, for once, wasn't going to be a problem. Freezing to death and drowning were more likely.

Dawn comes early in the Oregon June, but Anne and I were well ahead of it as we drove to Estacada, windshield wipers thumping and a southeast wind blowing hard enough to catch my attention. It wasn't a huge wind, but the Clackamas River runs westward out of the high Cascades, and I knew the canyon would pick it up and funnel it right at me. Nearby, the city of Portland was celebrating its annual Rose Festival, and Portlanders complain that it always rains during the event. That's not technically correct, but this year, they were definitely correct.

After registration, I bid adieu to Anne and boarded a bus, which decanted me up the canyon at a park, about 40 minutes before the start of the race. Normally, that's the ideal time, but this was a very small park, without even a picnic shelter in which to hide from the elements. There were only 200 runners in the race, and a substantial fraction of us wound up huddled in a grove of the biggest Douglas firs we could find. Like natural umbrellas, the downward sweeping limbs of these enormous trees can shed rain for a very long time, although eventually even they become waterlogged and start to drip. But at least they cut the wind.

Even with the small number of racers, there weren't enough portable toilets to go around, so runners were disappearing into the woods seeking their own private comfort stations. I jog-walked with a couple of friends, then stretched my calves, using one of those magnificent firs as support. Then, as well stretched out as I was going to get under these conditions, I returned to my Douglas-fir umbrella and stood in a cluster of other runners, trying to stay warm.

The Clackamas River Canyon is a 2,000-foot-deep gash where the river plunges from pool to pool between foaming rapids, flanked by hillsides outcropped with dark basalt. It's stunning terrain, and even after years of living in Oregon, I had never failed to appreciate it. It would be nice, though, if the rain would quit. A well-built asphalt road threads the length of the canyon, but it wouldn't be closed to traffic because there is no alternative route. Normally that wouldn't be a problem, but today was the beginning of fishing season, and we had been advised to keep alert. In Oregon, fishing is far more than a mere hobby, and we would definitely have company.

As the time ticked toward the start, it began to look as though the weather might comply with my wishes, though by race time it was still drizzling. Meanwhile, I contemplated strategy. The first mile was on one of the steeper downgrades, so I knew that everyone would go out fast. On a course like this, that's part of the race plan: you use the downgrades when you can, rather than holding back to a preordained pace. Still, it's possible to get pulled out too fast, so I needed to be careful.

When the gun sounded, the front-runners quickly split into two groups. I let the first one go and settled in with the second, which contained about eight other runners. We ran downhill like this for a couple of miles and then bounced partway back up through a series of curves. On the upgrade, my pack broke up, with some going on ahead and others dropping back. I was left with two young fellows who were apparently running together. They acknowledged my presence and asked what finish time I was looking for (an oft-asked question among strangers looking for a few miles' companionship).

But while I got quaint looks from both when I told them my target, they then ignored me and returned to their original conversation, which had something to do with fishing, and why on earth weren't they on the river, rather than putting themselves through a marathon. By the time I pulled away, at the eight-mile mark, I was as baffled by them as they had apparently been by me. Would people who looked that much like fit, seasoned runners really rather be standing on a riverbank? Maybe I had just not lived long enough in Oregon to understand, but I suspected that I could live here until I was 110 and still not fully understand fishermen.

For another mile, I ran alone—just me, the trees, the mountains, and the endlessly curving road. Then, on a relative straightaway, I spotted a tall man with graying hair. Wondering if he might be in my age group, I set about catching him, an occupation that took another six or seven minutes. When I finally came abreast, I slowed, and he introduced himself as Mel Pready. He wasn't my age—he was 10 years younger—and he had run even more marathons this year than I had, something like six or seven. Tomorrow, he was planning to do yet another in Coeur d'Alene, Idaho. And I thought I had a heavy racing schedule!

"How can you do that?" I asked.

"I'll drive up there as soon as this race is over," he said.

"But you'll have no rest!"

"It doesn't matter much 'coz I'm not trying to break any records."

I figured that running back-to-back marathons, with a 400-mile drive between them, had to be some kind of record in itself. I might have my own crazy streak, but I would never even dream of anything like that. And yet I know there are people who collect marathons the way others collect souvenir mugs or trucker caps. Mel is one of these, and he has done very well at it. Since 1995, I've seen him on several other occasions, and the last time we talked, his lifetime tally was close to 300. Still, as I pulled ahead of him and resumed my own record quest, I couldn't get the figures out of my head. Two marathons are 52.4 miles of racing in two days. That's about as much mileage as I ever ran in a week—and a lot more than in some weeks.

•  •  •

The rain had finally stopped and I was again on my own. The clouds thinned and enough sunlight made its way through to raise steam on the pavement and pick up the air temperature by several degrees. It wasn't hot; it was blessedly warm, and it felt good.

A corner or two later, I spied another group of runners and resolved to catch them. Like a lot of runners, I use other people to play little mental games with myself, wondering if it's someone I know, what the other runner's pace is, and whether I can catch him (or her).

At the start, we had been instructed to run on the left-hand shoulder, facing traffic (and, coincidentally, always on the more scenic side, close to the river). But the rain had made the shoulder soft and slow, and like most other runners, I was on the pavement. At the curves, I was also running the tangents, dodging back and forth across the road to shorten the distance by straightening out the bends as much as possible. This is accepted behavior on winding courses, and most are measured taking it into account. In Valencia, the blue line had automatically led me on the shortest route, but here I had to choose my own path.

Although there were many pickup trucks parked along the way, most of the fishermen had already reached their fishing holes. Traffic was therefore sparser than expected and cutting the corners was safe, as long as you kept your ears open. Rather than heavy fishing traffic, what we had was a very diligent policeman who drove back and forth along the course, shouting to the runners to stay to the left. The first time I saw him, I was one of the ones who got yelled at. On subsequent occasions I was on the proper side, though only by chance.

I caught the other runners, passed them, and was again on my own. The overcast had turned to patchy blue and the temperature was perfect, so I let the scenery envelop me and dull the minor aches in my limbs, all normal for this stage in a race. The rain had left an invigorating tang to the air, combined with a pleasant damp-earth smell rising from the wet soil. It was good to be cruising easily along on a suddenly beautiful morning, pondering my chances of making my goal but not overly anxious about whether I succeeded. I was living in the moment, surrounded by an aura of goodness and spirituality, flavored with a distinct sense of community from knowing that even though nobody else was in sight, I was sharing this experience with 199 kindred spirits. Simply being able to run at my age was a precious gift, and for the moment, relishing it was all that mattered. I again felt invincible—not in winning, but merely in being. I don't know whether other runners have such moments.

They don't always happen for me, but today I had an equanimity that was wondrously comfortable and satisfying. I rarely go to church; the outdoors is my church, and it is here that I make my communion.

I was now neither passing nor being passed and had been alone for some time except for occasional glimpses of fishermen down by the river. There is an old British film, *The Loneliness of the Long Distance Runner,* which I have not seen, based on a book of the same title that someday I probably should read. It had been made before I became a runner, and now as an actor turned runner, I pondered it. As an actor, would I have liked to be in it? As a runner, would I enjoy watching it? What would I have thought of it if I had seen it when it was made in 1962? And what exactly did the title mean?

I continued at an even pace, with each curve bringing new sights, new birdsongs, and occasional voices floating up from the river, unintelligible but comforting. Maybe fishermen weren't totally strange. Maybe they, like me, felt the magic of this wonderful morning, living for the moment as the river flowed by them as I now flowed through its canyon.

Rarely, on the longest straightaways, I saw other runners. The closest was a group of three about a half mile ahead. I didn't even consider trying to catch them. I was too enthralled by the divine solitude in which I was wrapped. Maybe this was *The Loneliness of the Long Distance Runner.* Someday I really did need to read that book. I still had many miles to go, but I had mercifully forgotten the relentless distance of the marathon, in which spiritual moments such as this can all too quickly be replaced by pain so nearly unbearable that finishing at all, let alone in a respectable time, seems well-nigh impossible.

I had come 18 miles now and was moving well. The long quest appeared finally over. In four prior attempts I had never felt this good or been this well on pace this far into the race.

• • •

A lot can happen in eight miles.

In the two hours since the race started, the wind was picking up, and there were fewer trees to block it. On some corners it had already been quite strong, slowing my progress even on downgrades. Now, at mile 19, a long upgrade presented itself, steep in places. I had been expecting it and knew that mile 20 would bring a solid downgrade, but I had not expected the wind to be here, too. In a mere mile and a half, life had gone from divine to miserable.

Desperately, I looked for mile 20, but it didn't come and didn't come, until finally, there it was, about 300 meters beyond the crest. I wondered if I was hitting the wall again, as I had in Houston, but for the moment, at least, what I had was a downgrade. I thought back to how, only a few miles earlier, I had been rhapsodizing about everything. The memory reenergized me, but I must not have looked good, because a runner now passed me—the first in at least 15 miles—and asked if I was OK.

"Yes, thank you," I said, telling him (and myself) that I had merely had to slow "a bit" for "a touch of a breather."

But I couldn't shake the tiredness. My calves cramped. I had to stop and lean against a telephone pole to stretch them out, just as, before the race, I had stretched against that big fir. Another runner passed by, also asking if everything was OK. I told him yes, which wasn't quite right, but there was nothing he could do about it, and I wasn't in any kind of life-threatening danger.

What I *was* concerned about was that if I tried to push through the cramps, I might pull a calf muscle, ruining not only the race but the rest of the running season. The moment I had stopped at the telephone pole, I had dropped all plans for a sub-3:00. I would baby my offending calves, finish the day as a training run, and go for the record some other time. Now it was only a matter of getting myself to the finish intact.

I stretched and rested for about three minutes. I had thought I might be stiff and sluggish when I again started running, but instead, I felt surprisingly lively. Even though I had to take three more 30-second stretch breaks, I caught and passed both of the runners who had earlier been solicitous of my health. One slapped me on the behind as I came by. "Good on yer, mate," he called. I didn't need to hear the accent to know where he was from. We ran together for a couple of hundred meters, and he told me that he was vacationing from Australia, visiting friends in Portland, and mixing sightseeing with racing. Even with my cramping calves, I thought it sounded like a pretty good holiday.

My finishing time ultimately proved only a few seconds slower than my races in Valencia and Kelowna. In fact, if I had only been able to run 6:56s down the long hill after mile 20, I would have had my three hours. In a race in which I had spent perhaps four and one-half minutes stretching, I had run 3:03:30.

## CHAPTER 12

# Port Cities

### Pancake Interlude: Estacada, Oregon—1995

When I review my training log from the days before and after the Clackamas Canyon Marathon, one thing stands out: in addition to my normal, detailed recording of all of my mile splits, I find the following diarylike entry: "158 pounds, too heavy! Lose six pounds, work out with weights—quads, hams, calves and upper body. Try again!"

The try-again plan was hatched over a massive breakfast as I was carbo-reloading after the race with Jack Keener, a friend who frequently wins the division five years younger than mine. Today, he had run only a 10K held in conjunction with the marathon, so he, Anne, and his wife, Betty, were primarily spectators as I worked my way through hearty portions of pancakes, eggs, bacon, hash browns, toast, and jelly. It may sound odd that I ate all of this shortly before complaining to my journal of being too heavy, but eating a substantial carbohydrate-and-protein meal after a marathon is one of the keys to rapid recovery. Ice baths are reputed to be another. I have done this a couple of times but did not find it enjoyable.

Out the window, marathoners were still heading for the finish, some looking fresh, others distinctly wilted.

"So," Jack said over his coffee, "When's your next marathon?"

"Funny you should ask. I'm thinking it will be Grandma's."

Grandma's was another familiar course, site of my first sub-3:00. It seemed a nice bookend to Clackamas, where I had run my most recent one—not to mention that fond memories of it might translate to good karma. "It's a week from Saturday," I added.

Jack was looking at me oddly, but it was Anne who spoke. "For goodness' sake, John! Shouldn't you rest up for something later in the year?"

I explained that actually, I had already signed up for Grandma's. I had done so at the same time I had signed up for Clackamas Canyon, under the theory that I might as well reserve a spot and that I would only truly go for broke at one of them. In support, I cited my theory that by taking all of those stretch breaks in today's final 6.2 miles, I had converted the experience into nothing more than a training run. "With lots of rest I can do it," I said.

Jack had finally found his tongue. "John," he said, "you just told us you thought Mel Pready was crazy. Now here you are, doing the same."

"Not quite," I countered. Mel was doing Clackamas and Coeur d'Alene on back-to-back days, with a 400-mile drive between. "I have two full weeks."

There is nothing like an argument to make me dig in my heels. "I'm on a roll," I said, once breakfast was finished. I was already beginning to feel restored. "I'm definitely going to do Grandma's."

## Copper Bottoms: San Francisco—1957

*"I'm sorry, you're just not right for the part."*

*"I'm sorry, your accent is too strong. The character's not supposed to be English."*

*"I'm sorry . . . "*

• • •

San Francisco was a much livelier musical center than Portland, but in my first weeks there, "I'm sorry" was all I heard. It didn't take much of that before I faced the perennial problem of out-of-work actors the world over. The money I had made in Chicago was gone. I had bills to pay, and I had to find some way to pay them, even if it had nothing to do with theater.

And so it was that I answered an ad for a door-to-door salesman. The ad led me to a seminar where I sat with a group of others in a hotel conference room, listening to a glib middle-aged man (probably another out-of-work actor) tell us how we could make tons of money selling stainless-steel cookware. "Jack over here is now a team manager," he said. "He gets commissions from the commissions of each person on his team. And Donald over there gets commissions from the commissions from the commissions, because he's the team manager's manager." The speaker himself was earning four or five commissions, and we could do the same if we had stick-to-itiveness. Of course, before we could stick to anything, we must buy a complete demonstration package that sold at retail for more than 600 dollars but that we could get for a mere 400 dollars.

Our instructor gave us all the relevant sales techniques, ranging from how best to gain entry to a family's home to the most reliable means of closing the sale. The presentation was slick and plausible, and I bought a demonstration kit and set out to make my fortune—or at least pay my bills. The very next day, I was given my own sales region.

I was living in Oakland with Anne's brother, and my selling area was to be close by. During the day, I was told, I should call on housewives, seeking to make appointments for the evening, when husband and wife would be able to share my presentation. I dutifully did so and made a few presentations using the dramatic technique we had been taught, which involved an attempt to frighten the would-be buyer with tales of how aluminum pots and pans caused cancer. Stainless steel was the only way to go.

The shiny steel pots with their beautiful copper bottoms were indeed very well made, and during my presentations, I laid them out on a purple cloth designed to show them to best advantage. They might even have been a worthwhile purchase had they been several hundred dollars cheaper and not sustaining the salesman, his team manager, the area manager, the regional manager, his manager, and so on.

I was an actor, but I could not lie to people who allowed me into their homes. I dropped the line about cancer and tried to sell the product on its merits as fine cookware. When at last I sold a set, I immediately felt guilty that the purchaser had paid too much. I asked the good lady several times if she really wanted it, all the time hoping she might change her mind, but she was adamant. She had been looking for new cookware, and this was the best she had seen. Then and there, I sold her my demonstration package and pronounced myself done with pots and pans, having made 200 dollars for four weeks' work. I was not cut out for this kind of commerce but did leave its employ with a clear conscience.

Returning to my real profession, I managed to get another job singing in an Italian restaurant. But it wasn't as upscale as the one in Chicago, and I didn't get any big tips. The pittance I *was* paid made it uneconomical to stay, so I abandoned California and went back to McMinnville.

# Farmboy: McMinnville, Oregon—1957

I had been in San Francisco only a few months, but by the time I got back to the Nortons' farm, Anne was no longer there. It was late summer, and she had moved to Roseburg, 200 miles south, where she was teaching high school English and speech. It felt as though I was no closer to her than I had been in San Francisco, but at least she wasn't so far away that she couldn't come back on weekends.

Meanwhile, I set about earning my keep as a farmhand.

Despite my years as a city lad, I enjoyed the agrarian life, perhaps because I never intended it as a permanent career. I learned to drive a tractor, mow and bale hay, feed and water livestock, change irrigation pipes, and generally become an all-purpose handyman. It was September, and there were always things to do.

In addition to growing crops, the Nortons raised turkeys. The chicks were housed in a specially heated and lighted shed, but when the birds were large enough to be classified as "young feeders," they were put out on the range— basically an eight-acre feedlot lined in turkey-proof fencing.

Scattered about the range were feed hoppers that had to be replenished daily. It was a chore I liked because I got to drive the tractor. Sitting atop the big machine, lumbering across the landscape, I would practice my songs, treating the turkeys to a daily dinner theater. In the restaurant in San Francisco, I'd sometimes had the depressing sense that Caruso could have been there and nobody would have cared. Here, it didn't matter that I had an audience for which dinner was the *only* thing that mattered.

Including the chicks in the incubation shed, there were five thousand turkeys. The range had a dozen feed stations that I would replenish from a large grain trailer towed behind the tractor, and as I sang my solos, I would be followed by a chorus of gobbling turkeys, eager for their food.

Dispensing the feed was a largely automated process involving a spiral drive that raised grain from the trailer to a chute that could be swung into position over each hopper. It was easy work but also dangerous because the spiral drive was operated by the tractor's power takeoff—a spinning coupling designed to harness the tractor's power for all manner of farm equipment.

There was a "proper" procedure for loading the feed stations. I would pull the trailer into position, climb down from the tractor, open the lid of the feed hopper, swing the chute into position, and then climb back onto the tractor. Only then would I shift the engine to a special gear that engaged the power takeoff. But like all proper procedures, it was cumbersome. I thought there surely had to be a more efficient way.

I had noticed that from the time I engaged the power takeoff, there was a 15-second delay before the first feed pellets emerged from the chute. If I moved quickly, there should be plenty of time to engage the power takeoff first and then jump off the tractor and swing the chute into alignment before the feed began to flow. I tried, and it worked. It was like cutting tangents on a winding racecourse: it was logical and efficient, and it saved a few seconds at each feed station—not to mention that it had the appealing element of being a contest against time to avoid spilling the feed.

One Sunday morning, when the Nortons were at church, I filled the trailer with grain, towed it to the range, and set about filling the feed hoppers, followed by the usual flock of turkeys. For some reason, they clustered more tightly than usual around the tractor, making it difficult to climb on and off. Still, I got through the first seven hoppers without incident, and at the eighth, I again took my now-usual shortcut of engaging the power takeoff before dismounting.

What happened next could have killed me or nipped my still-undiscovered running career in the bud 23 years before my first race. It was a big step to the ground, and there was no option but to put my foot close to the spinning menace of the power takeoff. As a former aircraft mechanic, I should have recognized how risky this was, but I had been having too much fun singing and driving the tractor to think about it. Now I stepped too close. In a flash, the coupling grabbed the cuff of my bluejeans and started to wind them up. Frantically, I reached for the shift lever, but it was too far away.

If the power takeoff had gotten a good grip on my jeans with the first revolution, I would have died right then. But as it spun, the jeans slipped, saving me from being instantly sucked in. With each revolution, however, the shaft tightened its grip, and I knew I was being inexorably drawn into the machinery.

Somehow, I managed to stay on my feet. I screamed for help, but with the Nortons at church, the only response was an increasingly agitated gobbling from the turkeys, whose numbers seemed to be multiplying.

Years later, one of America's top marathoners, a dairy farmer named Dick Beardsley, would suffer the same fate and end up barely alive, his leg shattered. Dick and I are now friends and have run a number of marathons together, but for him it was a slow, torturous recovery. I was luckier. Still on my feet, I braced as hard as I could and yanked, in a last, panicked effort to free my pants. Miraculously, something tore, not at the cuff but at the waist, and suddenly I was free, sprawling backward among hundreds of smelly turkeys as the power takeoff ate not only my jeans but also my shoes.

When the bomb fell in London, I never felt fear, never realized how close to death I had come. This time, I knew. The death I had avoided was still there, beating the remnants of my jeans against the ground in a rat-a-tat that told me exactly what had nearly befallen me.

In the adrenaline shock, I found it funny. Here was I, the great English tenor, standing in his underpants, bleeding, among what now appeared to be at least a thousand turkeys whose incessant gobbling was chastising me not because I had nearly killed myself but because I still hadn't filled the hopper.

The whole thing had happened so quickly that the grain wasn't yet spilling on the ground. I shut down the tractor to save the feed, but the turkeys would have to wait. The sudden loss of my pants had torn an enormous amount of skin from both legs, all the way from the groin to the knees. I was bleeding and oozing plasma, and I just *had* to get away from those stupid birds.

I limped back to the house wearing nothing but my underpants and socks (I had been working without a shirt), hoping no neighbor would see me. My immediate concern was to clean my wounds. Not bothering to remove what little clothing remained (the thought was simply too painful), I ran a tub of warm water, and while it filled, I tried to blot my wounds with toilet paper. It wasn't a smart move. Little bits of tissue stuck to the skin, adding a new layer to everything I had collected from the turkeys. There now being enough water in the tub, I climbed in, splashed it over the toilet-paper-shrouded wounds . . . and screamed.

Within moments, I was shivering uncontrollably and clearly starting to go into shock. I managed to get out of the bath, blotted my legs dry, put on a T-shirt and loose-fitting shorts, and waited for someone to come home. In the distance, I could still hear the sound of turkeys.

• • •

The emergency room was an experience best forgotten. I was swabbed, bandaged, injected, prescribed a pain medication, and told to come back daily for a month to have my dressings changed. It would be a year before I was completely pain free. Happily, nobody lectured me on my stupidity. Every farmer has nearly killed himself somehow or other, and the presumption was that this was one mistake I would never make again, so why bother talking about it?

If only runners learned from their mistakes as easily as farmers did.

# On the Shores of Gitche Gumee: Two Harbors, Minnesota—1995

*I keep an extremely detailed running log—a legacy of my days as an accountant for the RAF. The entry for my sixth attempt at the world record is as detailed as the others, but key phrases jump out:*

> *17 June 1995. Grandma's Marathon. Warm at start . . . Sang National Anthem . . . Mile six @ 39:55 = 6:39s . . . Mile 10 @ 1:08 = 6:48s . . . Drank well . . .*

*I can read other details, but the memory flows back . . .*

• • •

Grandma's is another course on which I could merely score an unofficial world's best. Its sins in the eyes of the record certifiers are twofold: there is a slight net downgrade, and it's point-to-point. Neither offers much hope of measurable assistance. The downgrade is trivial and confined to the first two miles, and the course runs southeasterly, into the prevailing summer winds. Just as the winds almost never blow down the canyon in the Cascades, summer northeasterlies are rare in the Midwest. Despite the lack of record certification, Grandma's is a very "honest" course.

My training plan was the same as for Clackamas except that this time I had an extra day: 14 instead of 13. I would focus on rest, rebuilding my energies, and sharpening my speed. There wasn't time for anything else.

By Thursday after Clackamas, my legs were no longer stiff, so I hit the track for some brisk 400s, all in the 88- to 83-second range. I stretched several times a day and abandoned my idea of losing weight. Keeping up my energy was more important. I also thought of the main pointer I now give to younger runners at racing clinics: good marathoners begin by committing to a program and then succeed by applying themselves to carrying it out. *Commitment* and *application*—those are my watchwords. I had committed to running Grandma's on two weeks' rest. Now I needed to apply myself to making it happen. I never questioned whether it was a rational goal.

Looking back on it, I can't believe I ran six marathons in five months. But I had committed myself to seeking the record, and since January, I had been applying myself to make it happen.

I ran 28 miles in the first week (and did a bit of cross-training on an exercise bicycle), then Anne and I flew to Minnesota a week early, taking the opportunity to spend time with our son Richard, who lived in Superior, Wisconsin. Once back in the Midwest, I didn't run for three days, limiting myself to bicycling with my grandson Alex, whose four-year-old legs weren't up to much.

I felt amazingly strong and rested so shortly after the Clackamas effort and was beginning to believe this might be the attempt that finally paid off. Three days before the race, I took my only run of the second week: a nine-miler that included eight 400s on a high school track, where I cut the pace down to 80 seconds.

My only serious mistake came the night before the race, when I ate a large, high-carbohydrate dinner too late in the evening. Carboloading is important because it coaxes the body to pack extra glycogen into the liver and muscles. Glycogen is a runner's highest-octane fuel, and you typically have enough to go about 20 miles before you're thrown back on other fuel sources, primarily fat. Carboloading is designed to help the body increase these reserves so that maybe you can go a wee bit faster in the final miles.

Normally, I like to eat 13 or 14 hours before the race, but this time, dinner was delayed until 9:30 or 10:00 P.M. Then I ate too much. The result was that I woke in the middle of the night sweaty and feeling bloated. Digestion requires energy, which must itself be replaced from the digested meal, and I feared that my overindulgence might not have given time for that replenishment to have occurred. Or maybe it was just prerace paranoia. I had previously run 35 marathons, but even the most experienced runners can sometimes fret like neophytes.

•   •   •

Nocturnal rumblings notwithstanding, I felt sharp enough in the morning. The race started in the village of Two Harbors (don't ask me where the harbors are; I never looked for them), then moved to a back road along the shore of Lake Superior, where on a clear day, you could see the skyline of Duluth rising beyond the long, curving shoreline. There are runners who hate courses where you can see where you're going from so far out. It intimidates them, as does the fact that the destination doesn't seem to get any closer. I just run the mile marks. The finish is the same distance away, whether you can see it or not.

From Richard's house, Two Harbors is a 40-minute drive, but we left before sunrise to avoid any risk of being caught in traffic. It was a calm morning, and as darkness changed to predawn glow, the lake's waters reflected indigo, blue, and green. It was the type of morning that makes me most appreciate the marathon not simply as my own race, but as a community celebration with the brotherhood of athletes—an extraordinary expression of the human spirit, shared (in this case) with eight thousand other people. It was also the type of morning that makes me nervous: a beautiful day, a beautiful course, an ambitious goal—not to mention that it seemed rather warm for so early in the morning.

Jogging through my warm-up routine, I allayed the jitters by warming up my voice. I had been asked to sing the national anthem, which was scheduled to precede the wheelchair start—itself a few minutes before the much larger pack of runners would toe the line. I love singing the anthem, with its wide vocal range and wondrous highs, but early morning is never the easiest time. Gigli once said he could hardly spit at that hour, let alone sing.

Normally, when I sing the anthem, I barely have time to get from the microphone to the starting line, although at least I get to start on the front rank with the elites because, singing, I'm right there beside them and have nowhere else to go. This time, the advance start of the wheelchairs gave me more time to shift from singing to running mode, but I still got to start in front, with the cleanest possible shot at my record.

I set off at what I thought was a 6:45 pace and was astonished to hear my time at the first marker: "Six-oh-eight." *What? Too fast!* However, we had descended much of what passes for the downgrade in Grandma's, and probably, that was part of the reason for my overfast time. Lake Superior was on our left, glinting in the morning light while the sun played coy behind delicate clouds.

I get cold easily, so I didn't really mind the temperature, which had been 64 degrees at the start. The warmth made me feel speedy, and I zipped through the next mile again too fast, clocking 6:18. *Not smart.* I reined in my pace a little more, at the same time trying to run with the relaxed gait that would carry me most efficiently forward. Around me, other runners were talking strategy, and every nerve in my body could sense the energy of their plans—a subtle connection of my work with theirs that left me gliding effortlessly forward. My word, I was feeling *good*!

Mile four brought the first spectators since Two Harbors, but their cheers were oddly weak, almost apologetic, as though fearful of disturbing our concentration. Maybe they were so few in number that, without crowd support, they were embarrassed to actually shout.

Thoughts like these are, for me, a major part of marathoning. My theory is that the race infuses the brain with extra blood that heightens awareness of even the tiniest events. A three-hour marathon is 10,800 seconds during each of which the brain is constantly absorbing miscellaneous bits of information. Little dips in the road . . . potholes to be avoided (*Wow, that one goes to China! I had forgotten what it was like to live in a climate where frost heaves wreck the roads each spring*) . . . paper cups on the roadside downstream of water stations (*Did I drink enough?*) . . . portable toilets (*Did I drink too much? Where's the next one, if I need it? What happens if I don't want to stop? Can I pee down my leg as the elites do? If I try, and succeed, I'll have to throw a cup of water over my body at the next water station so no one will suspect . . . Make sure it's not Gatorade or the next 20 miles will be rather sticky . . . Would that cause blisters? . . . Why am I thinking this? It's warm, my kidneys have shut down, and I'm not going to have to pee, anyway*). Stream-of-consciousness writers have nothing to teach a marathoner on the move.

Then comes a new, less-welcome thought. This isn't a record-certified course. If I set my record, it's not real; it won't truly count. Why am I doing this? Why not ease off, enjoy the outing, enjoy the people?

It is impossible to recount the string of such thoughts in a 26.2-mile race, and it would take three hours to do it, anyway. Information is being taken in all the time, assessed, reassessed, digested, deleted, debated, and rearranged— all while new (undoubtedly brilliant) ideas and (equally brilliant) strategies are clamoring for attention.

In normal conversation, when people my age cannot recall the name of something or someone, they often describe the experience as a "senior moment." I prefer to say that my "hard drive" is full. Perhaps it's because, in all of those marathons multiplied by 10,800 intensely lived seconds (plus hundreds of shorter races), I've stuffed it so full of random trivia that there is no room for anything else. Much of that trivia is just mental static that disappears from one step to the next. But much lingers and can be retrieved simply by glancing at my running log and setting that day's race memory on replay.

By now, the dominant mental exercise is mathematics. With each mile marker, I redo my pace arithmetic again and again, trying to ensure that I am not overrunning my goal, calculating for the 10th, 20th, and 100th times exactly how fast I have to go if I am to achieve my target. I hit mile six in 39:55—a 6:39 pace, still too fast. I am going to pay for this, but maybe I have enough time in the bank that it doesn't matter. A passing runner slaps me on the back and thanks me for my singing. I acknowledge him and then get back to pace calculations. I now have 90 seconds in the bank. I can run as slowly as 6:58s and still break 3:00. *That should be easy*, I think, but then I remember Lemon Drop Hill at mile 23. It has been years since I ran this course, and I try to remember how big it is. It's a silly name for a hill (lemon drop, how trivial—a tart confection no bigger than a teaspoon, but the people here fear it as though it were some alpine mountain shrouded in clouds). Just as the race itself is named for one restaurant, so the hill is supposedly named for an eatery (or is it a tavern?) that is (or was?) at the top.

Regardless of the details, Lemon Drop is a hill. Hills slow you down. But from the summit, it's flat or gently downhill all the way to the finish.

Meanwhile, the 6:39 pace feels good, so I continue putting time in the bank.

• • •

The crowds are growing, and now they aren't embarrassed about being too enthusiastic. Sometimes, runners and spectators trade banter. "Why don't you use some of that energy and join us? It's only 19 more miles!" says one wag to a particularly enthusiastic spectator. I have been running with this man and his buddies for three miles now, and he has kept everyone amused—a one-man show whose stage is the road.

"Too late," comes the answer. "I already did it as a training run."

I have no clue whether the spectator was telling the truth, but even our comedian has no comeback to that.

• • •

The temperature is now up to about 70 degrees, so I slow to grab a cup of Gatorade and walk several steps to imbibe. I am alternating drinks: water at one station, Gatorade at the next. The need for hydration is basic, but the science of energy-replacement drinks is hit and miss. Like many runners, I find that the sugar in Gatorade is helpful, but too much makes me feel blah. Years later, I will discover that a can of Slim-Fast or a similar "complete meal" drink allows me to sustain long training runs without tiring, but I have never tried it in competition. It could be done only at races where I would be allowed to cache my own special drinks at the elite-runners table, and there's too much danger I would be denied access to it by aid-station volunteers who have never heard of a 70-year-old elite.

Some of the runners around me are discussing the heat. With the temperature rising so rapidly and no cool lakeshore breeze to counteract it, they are expecting to be seven or eight minutes slow. I hope they're wrong. At mile 10, I am averaging 6:48s, not quite as fast as before, but I'm feeling as frisky as when the gun went off, and it takes discipline not to speed up.

• • •

Five miles later, it is noticeably warmer. I have left my comedian and his friend behind and am now with a group of seven, one of whom had been in London. As we share stories, he remembers me from an article in the *London Times*. He sympathizes with my having been tripped up there and wishes he could have been around to help me find a clearer path.

With only one-fourth as many runners here, I am in little danger of again being caught in the crush, but my new companion is himself target-ing three hours today and offers to pace me. In London, he had run slightly below 2:59.

• • •

Still, my pace keeps dropping. I am slower at mile 16 than at mile 10. At Grandma's, hypothermia is usually a bigger risk than sunstroke, but today, I have yet another overly warm race, and the heat is starting to take its toll.

We are nearing the outskirts of Duluth, and people are out on every lawn with garden hoses, offering to spray us down. The cool water is pleasant but comes at the price of soggy feet. At other races, that has left me with bloody blisters that usually burst before the end, sometimes turning my shoes red. But faced with a choice between blisters and giving up my shot at the record, the decision is easy.

My new group of companions has yet another clown, a young man of about 30 who helps me keep my mind off the foot woes that are sure to come before I complete the thirty thousand foot plants that comprise a three-hour marathon (an estimate; I have better ways to keep my mind occupied than to count them all). This comedian must also have fancied himself something of a gymnast. As we near the next aid station, he dashes ahead, does a pair of cartwheels, grabs a cup of Gatorade from a surprised volunteer, downs it, does two more cartwheels, and snags a cup of water farther down the line. I wonder if he has been doing this at every aid station. If I had that much energy, I could run a 2:50.

We have now covered 19 1/2 miles, and the 20th is coming up. When we get there, I discover I have slowed yet again. I am now averaging 7:01s and the heat is very much getting to me. Rather than having time in the bank, I now need to average 6:39s to hit 3:00—a very unlikely prospect. I have a bad sense of déjà vu.

Nor have we yet reached Lemon Drop Hill. I have almost no memory of it from my one and only other Grandma's; I had been in the process of running such a spectacular personal best that time that I could have charged up Mount Everest without noticing. But everyone else is dreading it. At least I have enough energy that even with the hill I can sustain a good pace to the end and finish in style, where the spectators will appreciate it. *Not that they will know me from Adam.* Or so I think. A mile later, I hear a voice from the crowd: "Hey, John Keston! Looking good! Go for it!" A bit later, I hear my name again. I had forgotten that my entry here has also drawn newspaper attention.

•  •  •

By mile 21, my companions have fallen silent. Like me, they are conserving every ounce of energy for the finish. It is my turn to play the wag. "Lemon Drop Hill is probably so sharp it will make our eyes water," I tell the cart-wheeling comedian. But even his heart is no longer in it because he has no comeback.

•  •  •

It's mile 22 now, and it has to be 80 degrees. But at least I know I will finish. I'd never actually failed to complete a marathon, but I always worry about it.

My companions and I are steadily passing other runners. Many are walking, some hobbling, but all look doggedly ahead to a finish line nobody can yet see. I love them, one and all, but I am always stunned by this phenomenon at the end of a race. All of these people went through the first six miles, 10 miles, 16 miles, and 20 miles faster than me, and now, even though I am slowing, I am running them down in droves. I may never be a master pacer, but at least I manage to tame my too-fast starts in time to be moving far better than average in the late miles.

•  •  •

Finally, Lemon Drop Hill is in sight. From the long straightaway leading to it, the hill looks like a wall rising above the branches of the trees lining the road. But that proves to be an illusion. By Oregon standards, Lemon Drop is barely a blip. I move into it . . . and practically before I realize what has happened, I'm at the top. Perhaps the fame of this hill stems from the contrast between 23 miles of dread and the euphoria that comes at the crest. Suddenly you know you've got the race licked (you really, truly *are* going to finish). You summon the energy for quick minicongratulations and hurrahs, then settle down to the reality that, assured of finishing or not, you've still got 20-odd minutes of work ahead of you.

I continue passing other runners. "Hey, mister singer," one says. "How old are you?"

Before I took up running, there were plenty of times I wanted everyone to think I was younger than I was. I now wear my years as a badge of honor. "You're an inspiration to us all, mister singer," I hear as I move on toward the finish.

The air surrounding each runner seems charged with expectation, elation, and joy (or is it merely incipient heatstroke?). Supporters line the pavement, calling names of loved ones. (How many times has my own family done the same for me?)

All of these runners are years younger than me. Undoubtedly, some are first-timers. For them, this marathon will be the ultimate achievement, a life-changing experience similar to the one that came to me so much later in my own life. What we cavalierly call "ordinary" life takes on new meaning the first time you cross that finish line, no matter how long it takes. You feel capable of tackling anything. The world seems a better place. Harmony and beauty abound. You love everyone. I have seen disappointed marathon *racers*, but never an unhappy *finisher*, in spite of bloody feet, sore muscles, and fatigue.

• • •

Mile 25, and we continue encouraging each other. "Go for it!" "Looking good!" "Only a mile to go!" "You're gonna do it!"

I had come here to set a record, and it is now abundantly obvious that I won't even get close. But the love I feel for all of these runners trumps the frustration of watching yet another shot at personal triumph slip from reach.

Now I am in downtown Duluth and there are shady spots between tall buildings. There is even the blessed hint of a breeze. I can hear the excitement of the finish as it passes, only a block or two to my left, and it doesn't matter that I still have to run a half mile beyond it, turn left, then left again, before I finally run toward that long-awaited banner. I can feel energy returning to my body, and my pace accelerates.

In the final blocks, the crowds are several rows deep and the bleachers are full. Festive music plays as an announcer calls out finishers' names and hometowns. I listen for mine but don't hear it, just as I can't hear Anne and Richard and the rest of my family adding their cheers to the crescendo of sound that ushers in the last few paces.

My time is 3:07:30—a far cry from what I expected but a course record that still stands. Reviewing my performance, I can find no grave mistakes other than the obvious one of running too many marathons too soon and the persistent bad luck of hot weather.

Still, it is time to quit chasing phantoms. Since London, I have gotten steadily slower. My 70th year is more than half over, and the marathon isn't the only race on the planet. Just as I have rarely stayed long in one place during much of my theatrical career, it is time for a change of running pace before winter comes and I am no longer 70.

## CHAPTER 13

# New Lessons

## *T*he Brooklyn Mafia: Eastern United States— 1959–60

The bandleader was the epitome of New Orleans jazz. A large, middle-aged white man with a full beard—rare in the 1950s—he puffed a ragged-looking cheroot and spoke in slow, rumbling tones, like gravel in a cement truck. "Can you sing jazz?"

Anne and I were having a late lunch on Bourbon Street—late enough (not entirely by accident) to meet musicians setting up for evening performances. After the incident with the turkeys, I had continued to assist on the Nortons' farm through the end of the harvest season and then had gone back to trying to earn a living with my voice. But I hadn't had much success, so I had decided to hit the road again. This time Anne had joined me, turning down a second year of teaching.

The whole thing wasn't exactly the smartest plan. Years later I would advise students to pick a city and stay put or at least contact local agents in advance and carry letters of recommendation. But I was as oblivious to that idea as, 36 years later, I would be to carrying water bottles between aid stations in the Valencia Marathon. Instead, I would spend more than a year rambling across the country, like a prospector always thinking his lucky strike is just over the horizon.

We started in Texas, where I looked up the big tipper from the Chicago restaurant. He arranged for me to sing at a private club, then, tipsy as ever, tried to pay me $500.

I had thought I was simply doing the show as a thank you. "I can't take that," I said. "It's too much."

We argued and settled on 100 dollars. Friends would later tell me I was crazy. In 1959, his offer was a lot of money, enough that Anne and I could have subsisted on it for months. As it was, I didn't want to spend the hundred. "It'll be our lucky hundred-dollar bill," I told Anne.

Next came New Orleans and the cheroot-smoking jazz musician. I had approached him simply to ask the name of a local agent, but the conversation quickly started to feel like an audition. I knew a bit of jazz, so Anne fetched my music from the car. He paged silently through it, drawing on the cheroot with steady *pfff*-ing sounds.

Eventually, he looked up. "I might have been able to use you, son," he said, "but you don't have enough in the way of standards for my gig. But can you sing 'My Funny Valentine' for me? I'd like to hear your sound."

I complied while he played the piano, ornamenting the instrumental interludes with improvisations that made me wish I had someone like him as a permanent accompanist. "Not bad," he said. He borrowed the club's phone and called an agent. It would prove to be the fastest I've ever gotten a gig: minutes later, we were fighting traffic up to Baton Rouge to a club that needed a new lead singer, *now*. Better, the gig ran for six nights and paid well enough to make us solvent for weeks. Maybe the hundred-dollar bill really was lucky.

Our next stop was Panama City, Florida, where we spent a week with a comedian we had met in Baton Rouge. We talked of doing a joint routine in which I sang and played straight man, somewhat as Dean Martin did for Jerry Lewis, but little came of it. Then it was on to Miami, where Anne and I finally had to spend the lucky hundred for a fleabag hotel. She was now pregnant, which thrilled us but meant that soon we were very much going to need money.

For several months, I worked my way up the Miami nightclub ladder. Anne worked retail during the Christmas rush and took whatever other short-term jobs she could find, and soon enough, we were out of the hotel and into an apartment.

In the meantime, I had developed another fan. His name was Jonas, and he owned a chain of clothing shops in New York and New England. He walked with a limp from a car accident, and I first became aware of him when he slapped his cane onto his table one night and ordered a raucous bunch nearby to shut up and listen to the singer. He was a good 20 years older than I, but we became friends, often meeting for breakfast.

There was only one drawback: Jonas was an alcoholic. He would start by asking the waitress for four glasses of orange juice. Then he would take a big sip from each and, when nobody was looking, top them off with vodka. "I used to drink whiskey," he confided, "but my doctor says it's not good for me." When the waitress returned, he would order pancakes with caviar and sour cream. If the restaurant had no caviar, he would ask that someone go buy some, tell them he'd pay for it, and tip extravagantly.

With a similar flair for the dramatic, he told me he knew a great agent back in New York. The agent managed Carol Channing, he said, and he and the agent were good buddies. If I would come to New York, we could all work together and make lots of money. It sounded good, and Jonas almost always got his caviar. That seemed a good omen.

A few weeks later, Anne and I followed him north. I was still the prospector, looking for gold.

•   •   •

Spring found us living on the third floor of a Brooklyn walk-up. Jonas's promises had proven to be nothing but an alcoholic will-o'-the-wisp, and I didn't even know if he knew Carol Channing's agent or had made the whole thing up. Either way, I was again in a new city, with no job and a wife too pregnant to work.

What I needed was a flesh-and-blood agent, not some mythical manager of the stars. It took six weeks, but I finally found one who booked me into a midpriced summer resort in the Catskill Mountains. It was a decent gig (the best on my entire eastward swing), working as MC and singer for a largely Jewish audience vacationing from the city. To accommodate them, I learned some Yiddish and Hebrew folk songs. Here I acquired yet another fan, Danny, who attended my performances much as Jonas had in Miami but without the vodka. Danny liked my Yiddish and Hebrew repertoire and suggested I change my name again—to Jocyl Kestenbaum.

Unfortunately, the gig meant I was in the Catskills when Anne's pregnancy came to term, though at least I was able to dash back to New York in time for the birth of Pamela, my first daughter. Better yet, the doctors soon cleared the two of them to travel, and they spent the rest of the summer with me.

Summer gigs eventually end, however, and three months later we were back in Brooklyn. That was when Danny tracked me down. "I can get you into the best nightclubs in New York," he said. "I have some good friends who can make it happen."

Something about that sounded suspicious. "What do you mean, 'good friends'?" I asked.

"Let's just call them 'the boys.' That's all you need to know."

That did not sound encouraging, especially when Danny told me he and the boys would take 80–90 percent of my earnings as their management fee. "Don't worry," he said. "You'll still make lots of money."

About the same time, I met another "promoter" who claimed to be some kind of union boss with an office he never seemed to visit. He wanted me to sing in a big Italian festival.

Meanwhile, Anne and baby Pamela had returned to Oregon to visit her parents. It was time to make a decision. I turned down $500 for the Italian festival, said another polite "no" to Danny, and returned to Oregon. I might have been a fool not to take the $500 tip from my Texan friend, but there are other types of help that only fools accept.

# Running in Circles: Mount Hood Community College—1995

Trying to get the body into peak athletic condition and keep it there has been compared to attempting to walk as close as possible to the edge of a precipice. The closer you get, the better your performance . . . until you get too close.

I had been walking this precipice now for six months, and, as always happens when you've done that for so long, you think you can keep it up forever. But another clock was ticking in addition to the steady slowdown from moving ever deeper into my age division, and I needed either to take an extended rest or to achieve my nonmarathon goals as soon as possible. For me, of course, that wasn't even a choice.

My immediate goal was the track.

Until I was in my upper sixties, I presumed track races were for kids and Olympians. For the rest of us, I thought the track was merely for training. I had certainly used it a lot for that. When I started serious racing, I immediately discovered *Runner's World* and read it from cover to cover, doing just about everything it suggested. Most of the writers were designing workouts for young, elite racers, but in my late fifties and early sixties, I tried them all. I particularly remember one involving 20 400-meter repeats, flat out. It's hard to do that without losing count, so I'd carried 20 pennies and dropped one with each lap.

When I moved to Oregon, though, I discovered a circuit of all-comers track races, some catering specifically to masters runners. I was a pretty good miler—good enough that my first world record was a single-age mark for 66-year-olds (5:27) in a street mile in Hibbing, Minnesota. A year later, a 5:33 mile at a meet in Portland was good enough for the 67-year-old outdoor track record.

The following year, I tried other events, ranging from 200 meters to 10,000 meters. I loved the atmosphere of small meets, where you can compete in multiple races (I have done as many as five in a day). I liked the excitement of running in a tight pack. I loved the electronic timing, which records everything to the hundredth of a second, even in events where such precision hardly matters. And I particularly enjoyed running on a well-built track. Unlike the roads, the track is perfectly level, and its rubberized material adds enough spring to your stride that it feels as though you are floating. There is a reason why track and road records are separate.

But the track season is short, and by the time I got back from Grandma's, there was barely a month left. A week after the marathon, I entered one of the bigger masters meets and ran five races in two days, totaling nearly 13 miles. The previous year, at age 69, I had added four more marks to my collection of single-age track records, but now I wanted at least one of the big prizes: a world age-group record.

My best distance in that meet was the mile, but I was at least 15 seconds too slow. Partly that was because I had run so many marathons in rapid-fire succession. But I also needed to adjust my training for shorter, faster distances.

Five days later, I ran the 1,500 in a regional meet and did better. My time was 5:15.51, equivalent to a 5:39 mile. I was in the ballpark.

The next weekend, I went for it. It was the State Games of Oregon, a kind of statewide mini-Olympics. The masters races were at Mount Hood Community College, which sports a world-class stadium a few miles from the base of its namesake mountain. There was only one problem. The scheduled race was the 1,500, not the mile. And while there is only 109 meters difference between the two distances, there is a world of difference in the records, because the mile is run far less frequently. In the jargon of runners, the mile is a relatively "soft" record and therefore the better target.

I talked to the meet officials, and they were happy to oblige me by changing the distance. But unless the rest of the field went along with it, it would be to no avail because, they said, for an event to count toward a world record, there had to be at least five people in the race. Why (or even if they were correct), I don't know. Decades earlier, this rule hadn't applied when Roger Bannister broke the 4:00 mile. It's one of those pronouncements you simply accept as the way things are done.

Two younger masters offered to pace me, but we still needed two other people, so we crossed our fingers and spread the word. Happily, the three of us had lots of friends. By race day, seven runners were signed up. Whatever happened would be official.

When the gun went off, I tucked in behind one of my pacers. The other ran beside me, in lane two.

People my age often complain about how time seems to speed up with each year. But there is nothing to stop it (at least temporarily) like running an all-out mile. The first lap always feels unsustainably fast. By the last one, it's amazing how far a quarter mile has become and how slowly those last seconds creep by.

Now, though, I not only had company, but the whole way, one of my rabbits kept up a running commentary: "Good job, John; you're on pace." "Pump those arms!" On the final straightaway, he called to the one ahead of me to get out of the way. "Kick it in, John!" he called. "Go on! Go!"

And so I did. I ran 5:34.03 (again, those luscious hundredths of a second that say that this is not the same thing as a 5:34.04 or a 5:34.02). It should have been a record, but the number never made it into the books.

When I asked why, I was told that while the time was indeed the fastest ever scored on an outdoor track by a 70- to 74-year-old, someone had run two seconds faster at an indoor meet earlier that year. In theory, indoor and outdoor track are distinct pursuits. Outdoor track is run on a 400-meter track under whatever conditions nature provides; indoor track is run on shorter (and sometimes quite odd-sized) tracks with banked corners and an indoor climate. At the time, I had never run indoor track, but when I later took it up, I found that the controlled climate and banked corners made me faster. But the conventional wisdom is that all of those extra turns slow you down, and the powers that be had concluded they weren't going to update the outdoor record unless it was faster than the indoor one.

I felt robbed. It made no sense, because the older mark, slower yet, still stood. But argue as I might, I couldn't get my name in the books. Nobody questioned that I had run 5:34. Nobody questioned that it was the fastest ever. They just weren't going to count it, and that was the way it was.

Could I have found another half second per lap had I known I needed it? Who knows? I was by no means the first to lose a record to the office politics of the record keepers and won't be the last. Meanwhile, I was still successfully walking my precipice, with plenty of additional races ahead.

## Opera at Last: Oregon, Indiana—1960–63

Anne and I were again living near her parents' farm—back where we had started, having done nothing but spin our wheels. At least I had avoided the type of success that comes from selling your soul to La Cosa Nostra.

Anne found a teaching job, nearby this time, and I enrolled in the music department at nearby Linfield College, a liberal arts school of three thousand that occupies much of the center of town. At 35, I still had no formal schooling, though I'd had years of private voice lessons and more experience than all the other students combined.

Voice majors were required to participate in the college choir, but the professors gave me a special position as male soloist and kept me busy with concerts and the lead role in a musical. But one of them thought I was selling myself short. "Why on earth are you at Linfield?" he asked. His name was Warren Baker, and he taught brass instruments, not voice. "You should be at Indiana."

Professor Baker was a proud Indiana University alumnus, but he wasn't speaking merely from Hoosier pride. Indiana had the best opera department in the country. Nevertheless, I had no real desire to go. The main reason I was taking classes was that I was tired of the road, and McMinnville provided a good place for Anne, baby Pamela, and me to recoup. Taking courses was fun and I might learn something useful.

Professor Baker, though, insisted that the most useful thing I could do would be to complete my studies—at Indiana.

A week later, early on a Saturday morning, the phone rang.

It was Indiana's dean of music. "I hear you have a good tenor voice," he said, "and are thinking of transferring."

I told him I wasn't. But IU's music department had earned its fame by recruiting singers the same way the sports teams recruited athletes. "I can make it worth your while," he said.

It took me a moment to realize he was talking about a scholarship—exactly what I had wanted from the British government all those years before. "Can you record a few songs and send a tape as soon as possible?" he added.

At Linfield I had easy access to tape recorders and sound rooms. The results weren't as polished as my MGM record (which wasn't appropriate because he needed opera, not pop songs), but he wasn't planning to put it on the radio. Nor could I have asked for a better way to audition. Rather than standing nervously before an audition director, it felt just like practice—with the knowledge that if I didn't like the result, I could simply push "erase" and nobody but my accompanist would ever know. I recorded several arias from my nightclub repertoire and sent the tape special delivery.

Thus it was that the following August, Anne, baby Pamela, and I wound up in Indiana. My official title was teaching assistant, but my real work was performing. At long last, I was no longer standing on Gigli's doorstep dreaming of opera. I was being paid to sing it, and doing so in America's most prestigious academic setting. Over the course of two years, I would sing Don Jose in *Carmen,* as well as the leading tenor roles in *Forza del Destino, Don Carlos, The Darkened City, Cavalleria Rusticana, The Scarlet Letter*, and Gilbert and Sullivan's *Ruddigore.*

Teaching assistants aren't paid a lot—certainly not enough for a 37-year-old family man. So I took a second job, driving to Indianapolis every Sunday as a soloist for a large church. Anne found a teaching job about 50 miles away.

It was the most financially solvent I had ever been but also extremely stressful. I loved every moment on the stage, but between the teaching, taking classes, singing on Sundays, and rehearsing one opera while performing another, I was working 14-hour days.

Looking for a way to relieve the stress, I turned to exercise—the beginning of a habit I would maintain until I retired from both full-time stress and full-time performing. I could have picked any form of exercise, but Indiana is at least as famed for turning out Olympic swimmers as for turning out opera singers. Inspired by them, I hit the pool for an hour each weekday, figuring the lung development wouldn't hurt my singing, anyway.

Finally, summer came, and the high-intensity grind abated. I needed to relax, but it was also vital to keep the money coming in, so my friend Fulton Gallagher and I took a job cleaning married-student housing for next fall's students.

Fulton was a jovial baritone with whom I had done a couple of operas. He was working on his PhD in voice and at 27 was enough older than the average student that he and I were natural companions. We were both married and parents of two-year-olds, so our families often did things together.

That summer was one of the few times I would have liked to have been the bricklayer, carpenter, or concrete worker the British government had tried to make me into. Toting bricks is good, physical labor. But instead of that, Fulton and I spent three months cleaning ovens—not all that much stress, but far too much ammonia.

In addition to Fulton and me, our crew included a Pakistani student who was having trouble with the language. He was a nice guy, so we took it upon ourselves to help him, also teaching him a few words not found in his textbooks. Learning any new language, there is always some sound that trips you up. For English speakers, it's the *r* in French and Italian; for Italians, it's the *h* sound. This young man's Waterloo was *f*, especially when it came at the start of a word. It would come out *p*, so that "flat" became "plat" and "forest" was "porest." Determined to help him master this stubborn consonant, I wracked my brain for an appropriate tongue twister. Once I found it, I would greet him at each rest break by slowly and painstakingly repeating it: "four hundred forty-four fresh fish."

When the inevitable reply came, "Pour hundred porty-por presh pish," I would lean so close that he could almost feel the breeze of the English *f*: "Ff-four hundred ffforty-fffour fffresh fffish." But for weeks, all I got back was, "Pour hundred porty-por presh pish."

I had just about given up when one morning he spoke first. Putting his face close to mine, he looked at me intently and exclaimed: "Leesten, John, please, leesten, leesten!" Then as deliberately as I had drilled him, he articulated, "Fffour hundred ffforty-fffour fffresh fffish."

He grinned triumphantly. "Pucking good, eh?"

• • •

Then I was into more 14-hour days and my second year of studies.

In the spring of 1963, I received a letter from my father. "Can you come visit?" he asked. He and my mother were nearly 70 and I hadn't seen them—or Anthony, Michael, or Philip—for nearly eight years. It wasn't that I didn't want to; it was the prohibitive price of transatlantic airfares. You could buy a car in those days for the cost of a round-trip.

We still couldn't afford to go by air, especially not if I wanted Anne and Pamela to come with me. But after two years of teaching, singing, and cleaning ovens, we could afford the boat. That would take a week each way, plus a few more days traveling to and from the port. If we were going to spend that much time traveling, I figured we might as well do it right. So we packed up and set off for a summer in England.

# Over the Edge: Portland, Oregon—1995

In early August, I'd had another chance to be sworn in as a U.S. citizen, and this time I was in town to do it. Over the years, I had posted several times that would have been American records had I been officially American. Now, before my citizenship was two weeks old, I made a go for a real American record at a 12K road race called the Spirit of Springfield.

The 12K is another distance that is not widely run, though it's relatively popular in the Northwest. The world record was out of reach, but earlier this year, on a hilly course at an elevation of nearly 2,000 feet, I had run a time that would have been an American age-group record. I figured I ought to be able to do it again, especially on an easier course.

The race proved to be flat, distance certified, and as fast as could be wished. I ran steady 6:23s for a 47:36 finish, beating the old U.S. mark by more than a minute. But then I was robbed again. As far as I could tell, everything about this course qualified for a formal record. But USA Track & Field never credited me with it. When I made inquiries, the best I got was something about "lack of confirmation." Apparently, the race director never sent in the official results. I secured a copy (this was before widespread use of the Internet) and submitted them myself. But apparently that wasn't good enough.

Eventually I gave up. The 12K would have been a nice mark, but like the mile, it had been a soft record, one I had attempted to "cherry-pick"—another consolation prize for my failure to get the big one, the marathon.

Luckily, I'd had a third target that summer, a distance everyone takes seriously: the 3,000 meters.

The race was in Eugene, at Hayward Field. It was an all-ages event called, simply enough, the All-Comers Meet.

The 3,000 looked like an obvious target. A few weeks before, at the meet where I'd run my supposed-world-record mile, I had narrowly missed the world record for it. And that was after I had run an all-out mile. I figured that if I focused solely on the 3,000, I had a good shot.

The All-Comers Meet wasn't a large event, but it was sufficiently official for the results to count . . . as long as the requisite number of people were in the race. To ensure that (and to save time), the 3,000 and 5,000 were combined, with a joint start, set for 7 P.M.

The experts say you're faster in evening races because your body has had all day to warm up. But jogging through my warm-ups, that seemed dubious. I didn't feel fast; I felt dreadful. Still, I was there to make the attempt, so I made my way to the start, where I asked some of the younger fellows how fast they intended to go. I found two in the right pace range and mentally designated them as my rabbits.

Even when your warm-up feels sluggish, something magical happens at the sound of the gun. I've experienced this enough that I should expect it, but it always comes as a surprise. In the brief time it took to surge into action, I went from feeling dreadful to feeling like an athlete and soon was floating across the track as though I really belonged there.

I was floating so well that five or six laps into the race, I had dropped both of my rabbits. In their place, I had caught a 17-year-old boy. He was running smoothly at just about the right pace, so I stayed with him until in the final straight he kicked into a gear I couldn't match. But it didn't matter because I had my world record: 10:51. It might not have been a marathon, but it was an age-division record, the biggest prize I had ever snagged. And this time, it actually got ratified.

• • •

The pain had been there for a week, but with the help of ice and aspirin, I had been able to train through it. I thought it might be plantar fasciitis, a strain of the big ligament that runs beneath the arch of the foot. But with the help of ice and aspirin, it seemed to be getting better.

Counting track events, I had run 37 races so far this year. Now, with the cool of fall fast approaching, I was hoping for better times yet, after a summer of heavy training.

My next target was Lynn's Run, a small 5K designed to raise money for a cause I no longer remember. During the summer, I had run a pair of 5Ks at 19:14 and 19:21, and now I was determined to get below 19:00—not a world record but a good staging point for making a try later in the fall.

During Lynn's Run, the foot hurt every step of the way, but despite the pain, I was running well. Then, about a half mile from the end, I felt a sudden clicking sensation in the heel, followed by a sharp pain. I should have quit, though the damage, most likely, was already done. But I had never pulled out of a race and couldn't imagine doing so. With a mere 800 meters to go, I slowed my pace, then slowed it again. I lost a full minute, most of it in the final 200 meters, limping in scarcely faster than a walk, barely breaking 20:00.

• • •

Lynn's Run brought the streak to an end. The nagging pain in my heel had been a stress fracture, and the snap during the race had been from that hairline-crack separating into a full-blown break. My 1995 racing season was over.

# Ascending Star

*F*rom *Phoebe* to *Folderols*: England—1963

Our "summer" in England lasted more than 11 years. Reuniting with my parents and my three boys was wonderful. Even Mariolina and I found new common ground as ex-spouses and eventually friends. Years later, she and I are still in contact, and during those 11 years, my two sets of children took to each other quickly and interacted as well as their age differences would allow. Even Mariolina and Anne got along well enough, a tribute to both of them.

Flush with the joy of these pleasant events, I couldn't resist buying a copy of *Stage* to see what was going on in my old city. From that, it was an easy step to talking to an agent and auditioning for a couple of roles. Somewhat to my surprise, I was accepted for one of them: a musical called *Dear Miss Phoebe*, based on a play by James Barrie, author of *Peter Pan*. Suddenly, any thoughts of going back to Indiana to finish my degree were put on hold.

The play went through the usual rehearsals, toured the provinces, and came back to London . . . where it died in about three weeks. Such is the fate of most new plays. But I now had connections. I got a role in a Christmas show that garnered some of the best reviews I've ever had. I then took work with a summer revue called the *Folderols*.

I'm not sure I realized it, but I was no longer a starving actor. I was an established performer, able to keep busy enough to support my family, which was again growing. John was born in 1964, followed by Richard in 1967.

Anne and the children continued to live in the country, where she carried on teaching between babies. I joined them as often as possible, though the life of a touring performer kept me away more than I liked. Still, I had finally achieved a true life in the theater.

## Cable Street Redux: London—1996

Dreams die hard. Even though, after Grandma's, I had sworn off new attempts on the marathon world record, some back corner of my mind continued to think that maybe, just maybe, I wasn't too old. I hadn't formed a conscious plan to make a new assault on the record, but as shorter-distance successes had mounted during the following summer, the idea gathered momentum.

A fractured heel was a major setback. I was walking again within 11 days, but a broken bone takes weeks to heal, and recovering your stamina takes weeks more after that. Then it takes forever for your speed to come back. On a midnight 5K on New Year's Eve, I ran 20:57, breaking 21:00 only at the cost of a furious sprint. Then I ran a half-marathon at 7:09s: way too slow. I took three months off from racing and scored 51:10 in a small 12K—nearly 30 seconds a mile slower than my never-ratified American record.

Somehow, I convinced myself that this made me ready. The London Marathon was the course on which I had come closest to the record the previous year, so I booked a flight and resolved to give it another try.

• • •

For the weeks leading up to the race, my training diary tells a frightening tale. If sheer training volume could have gotten me my goal, I would surely have made it. Three weeks before the marathon, I ran an 82-mile week. "New regime to get really strong for a crack at WR," says my diary. On one 20-miler I never ran slower than 7:18s. The following day I ran 11.5 miles, some at a 6:26 pace.

Reading these figures, there is only one conclusion: I had gone insane. At least I tapered nicely. The following week I ran only 50 miles, and the one after that, 30.

Then came the race. This time, I didn't sit forever in the senior men's tent, shivering. I got to the start at a more reasonable hour with my son Tony, who was also doing the race. He had not yet broken 40:00 for 10K and had no hope of keeping up with me if I was in world-record shape, but as it turned out, it didn't matter.

Again, my training log says it all.

Mile 1: 6:56 (felt horrible)

Mile 2: 6:40

Mile 3: 6:38

Mile 4: 6:32 (too fast; out of breath and exhausted)

Mile 5: 7:12 (heart rate 152)

Miles 6-19: 7:08 to 7:45

Mile 20: stopped for Tony to use the porta-potty; 9:35.

Miles 21-26: walked at water stops and later stopped to stretch. Considered dropping out, but Tony kept me going. Temperature at finish: somewhere between 79 degrees and 82 degrees F.

Eventually, Tony pulled away and ran 3:18:53. Max Jones went by me in the final mile and ran 3:20:17. I ran 3:21:04. "Hardest marathon ever!!!" said my training log—the triple exclamation points seeming to leap from the page. Then the log proceeds to diagnose what had gone wrong:

Not enough speed work. Not enough 20-plus milers. Too much food and drink. Gained 10 lbs in England in 10 days.

The latter is a rather amazing figure (possibly the result of cutting back from 82 miles per week without adjusting my appetite), but the most amazing thing was what my diary doesn't say. Nowhere does it mention that I was attempting to run a world-record marathon less than seven months after a severe stress fracture. No number of 20-milers, dieting, and cool weather would have overcome that.

# King of Commercials: England—1965–74

*"Well, glory be, it's the king of commercials."*
  *"Hey John, I think I saw you three times last night."*
  *"Were you the man from Singapore?"*
  *"Dad, the kids at school keep asking if you're really the Toffee Crisp man."*

• • •

I got into commercials by accident: simply as something my agent saw as a way to pay the bills. But by 1966 it had become my bread and butter. They were lucrative, fun, and easy. Most were perfect little comedy sketches where I got to play the type of character you never get enough chances to play on stage. Once, I had five commercials, for as many products, playing simultaneously.

In the Toffee Crisp commercial, I was in a railway station, dressed in Edwardian style, preparing to board a train. A ticket collector reaches to punch my ticket, notices the candy, and sings (to the tune of the classic song), "Pardon me, sir, is that a Toffee Crisp you choo choo?"

My Singapore role was as a British businessman having dealings in Singapore. A customer invites me to his home for dinner. But what special dinner should the family serve? Uncle Ben's Rice.

My most successful commercial aired only once. In it, I played a sheik who watches his lady ride off into the sunset on a white horse. Forlorn, he retires to an ornate tent, singing "One Alone" from the 1920s musical *Desert Song*. But what can he do for a meal, now that he's on his own? The answer, of course, is the product being advertised: a Birds Eye frozen dinner for one.

I loved the music, the costume, and the setting. But what the director really wanted were big clouds of steam when I opened that hot meal. When we failed to get enough, he arranged for a nicotine-addict stagehand to peel back a corner before each take and blow cigarette smoke beneath it, via a straw.

The commercial was never intended to advertise the product. Rather, it was created for submission to the Cannes Film Festival, where it won the prize for best black-and-white commercial. The only reason it aired at all was to qualify for the competition as a bona fide commercial.

Another time, I got to drive a sports car. The ad was for Dunlop Tires, and at the outset I was asked whether I could drive fast. For actors who want steady employment, the answer to such questions is always "of course." So we went to Rome, where I drove laps around the Coliseum while they filmed the car and the tires. Then we headed onto the autostrada—the Italian equivalent to Germany's no-speed-limit autobahn. "You've got to tromp on it, John," the director said.

Today, I'm sure, such things would be done with some kind of special effect. But that wasn't possible in the early '70s, so I tromped obligingly. Too obligingly, it turned out. The cameraman trying to shoot over my shoulder was too terrified to shoot properly, and the director had to take the camera and film in his stead. At peak, I hit 130 miles per hour. Thankfully, the tires were as good as claimed.

• • •

In addition to commercials, I did supporting parts for television. One time, I was asked whether I could ride a horse, fast. It was a period piece, and in the relevant scene I was to gallop up to an inn with my cape flying behind. Horseback riding is one of those skills you definitely want on your resumé, so I had been taking lessons from young Pamela's riding teacher. But for this, I needed something better. Our country home was in an area where steeplechase horses were trained, so one day I went to a racing stable and talked to the head boy, explaining that I was an actor who needed to learn how to ride fast.

"I can help with that," he said.

In British racing, a "boy" is a stable hand, and many are jockeys. He put me on a "pacer" (a horse used to help train the fleeter, high-priced mounts) and took me to the downs for a gallop. "Just squeeze him gently," he said, once we were on a likely looking straightaway.

The horse sped up.

"Now, give him a sharp kick."

The horse took off as though shot from a cannon. The autostrada might have been faster, but charging headlong on a racehorse at 30 or 40 miles per hour is a lot more alarming. We tore across the downs, with me trying desperately not to fall off. Ahead lay an enormous hedge, probably six or seven feet tall, and the horse was heading straight toward it with no apparent intention of braking. It crossed my mind that the animal might think I wanted it to leap the hedge. That was something I most emphatically did not want. My role said nothing of leaping over hedges, and there are skills that aren't worth the risk of acquiring, anyway. "Whoa," I called, pulling back on the reins as hard as I could. "Whoa, whoa, whoa!" Eventually the horse stopped, practically nose to nose with the hedge. It seemed disappointed, but I didn't care. I was sure I had been about to die.

"What did you think of that?" the head boy said, reining in beside me.

Part of acting is the ability to keep your aplomb, even when it's trying to desert you. "That was good," I said. Then I added something more truthful. "I don't think I'm going to have to go that fast for the camera."

# Eighth Attempt: Back in the Hills, Kelowna, B.C.— 1996

Following the London Marathon, I faced the same problem I had faced in 1995: I wanted to race again as soon as possible, but there were limited options in May. Having been baked for two years in a row in London, though, I was looking to go north, so now I accepted the invitation issued the previous year to come back to Kelowna.

The course had been changed to eliminate the hills, and I hoped that would be all it would take to put me over the top. Besides, I had really liked the people and their beautiful valley, and the race organizers were nearly as eager to have me break a record on their course as I was to do it.

Before going to Canada, though, I got a chance to carry the Olympic torch. It was the summer of the Atlanta Olympics, and the flame was wending its way to Georgia via a circuitous route that came within a few miles of my home.

Being asked to carry the torch was a surprise; I never even found out who nominated me. I only carried it a quarter mile, at a slow jog with a high school girl, but it was a remarkably moving experience, uniting me across time with everyone who had striven so hard for excellence. Physically, the inspiration was no substitute for a younger, better-healed body. But psychologically? That was a different matter.

• • •

Kelowna was four weeks after London, and my training was much as before: lots of miles, many of them fast. I started at what I thought was a comfortable pace, but as the minutes went by, there was no sign of the one-mile mark: my usual reality check against going out too fast. Nor could I find a two-mile mark when the time should have come for that. It wasn't until five kilometers into the race that I found the first distance marker, which told me I had run those first 3.1 miles in 20:36. A quick calculation translated that into 6:38 per mile—way too fast. I dialed my pace back a bit, but there were no more distance marks for the next 20-plus minutes, when I crossed the 10-kilometer mark in 41:32—a 6:42 average pace, still too fast. After that, there were no marks whatsoever. The race had a new director this year, and for some reason he had chosen to mark the course only at those two locations.

I ran on without pace feedback for a dozen miles more or so. Then everything fell apart. Perhaps I was still going too fast. Or maybe it was the lingering effects of a cold I had gotten shortly after London. Whatever the cause, about 18 or 19 miles into the race, I was forced into the first of several walk/jog breaks.

The record obviously lost, I pressed on as best I could. My time was 3:11:46, nearly nine minutes slower than the year before. Still, it was nearly

10 minutes better than I had done in London. At least I was moving in the right direction.

## Sweet Charity: London, 1968–69

By the time I had been back in England for five years, I had the credentials to audition for major roles. One that caught my eye was Vittorio Vidal in a musical comedy called *Sweet Charity*. The story was by Neil Simon and the music by Cy Coleman and Dorothy Fields, all three of whom were theatrical legends.

It tells of Charity, a dance-hall girl with a heart of gold but terrible taste in men. Early in the show she meets Vittorio, an Italian film star who has just had a highly public fight with his girlfriend, and they spend an innocent evening in his palatial flat. Vittorio is more than a bit of a rake, but he treats her better than any man in her past. He is also a delightfully flamboyant character and one of the play's three leads (in the later movie version, he would be played by Ricardo Montalban). The show had at least two songs that are still well known: "Hey, Big Spender," and "If My Friends Could See Me Now" and while Vittorio isn't in either of them, he does have a to-die-for tenor solo called "Too Many Tomorrows." If there was ever a part made for me, this was it. I secured the audition easily enough—only to be told, "Sorry, you're too old."

I was stunned. I wasn't yet 45, and in real theatrical life, people like Vittorio aren't kids. Besides, I looked young.

I managed to get a second shot at the audition, but by that time someone the "right" age had been found, even though he didn't look Italian. It was frustrating, but there wasn't much I could do about it except look for other work.

Luckily, I hadn't found any when I got a phone call from a friend who was a dancer in the show. I asked him how it was going, though I wasn't sure I wanted to know. I knew he was going to say "swimmingly" or words to that effect, making me feel all the more frustrated at not being part of it.

And at first, that's what he said. But then he surprised me. "Remember that chap who got the role you wanted? Well, he can't sing very well and can't act Italian. He's either been sacked or is about to be sacked."

"What?"

He started to elaborate, but I shut him off. "Hang up," I said. "Now!"

As soon as I heard the click, I was dialing my agent. "Give me a few minutes," she said, "but stand by the phone." Minutes later, she called back. "You've got an audition at 1 P.M."

It was now 11:15—barely time to warm up my voice and get to the theater. "I'll be there," I said.

Luckily, I was in town, not out at our country house with Anne. I dressed quickly, warbling through some scales as I did so, and then headed for the theater. Despite the rush, I did my best to prepare a good entrance. I was dressed in a suit and my best overcoat, smoking a pipe, and wearing a trilby in the hope that I would look very swish and Italian. When I got there, someone gave me a script and introduced me to Juliet Prowse, who would be playing Charity.

Musical theater is odd because while the songs are crucial, people who call themselves "singers" are looked down upon. It's better to be known as an actor who, if necessary, can carry a tune. So even though Juliet had one of the great voices on the stage and we were in the company of a piano, we began with a read-through of selected portions of the script: an acting audition, not a musical one. Even when asked if I could sing, I downplayed it. "A bit," I said, because admitting I was classically trained would be the kiss of death.

The read-through went well. "Great accent," Cy Coleman said. Neil Simon was also in attendance. "Very good," he said. "Very authentic." "How could they have thought you were too old?" added Dorothy Fields, Coleman's cowriter. Then they told me to wait. "We've got three or four other people to hear," Simon said.

Rather than simply twiddling my thumbs, I wandered around the rehearsal facilities looking for a pianist, so I could practice that to-die-for solo. Of course, I still had to behave like an actor, not a singer, so I was nonchalant: "I understand that there's a song this character has to sing."

I had never actually seen the music before, but I've always been a quick study—and it really was as great a song as I had hoped. Then Coleman joined us again.

The great advantage of this rushed audition was that there had been no time for nerves. I had known all along that the part was perfect for me, and now I was auditioning for the creative geniuses behind the show, not some audition director fixated on a preconceived vision of the character's age.

By the time I finished singing, the job was mine. "A bit," Neil Simon said. "You call that singing 'a bit'?"

• • •

Juliet and I began rehearsing that very day. Three days later, we did a scene together live, on a late-night television show that filled the same niche in England that David Letterman's does today in the United States. Three days after that, we had our formal opening.

I had been preparing for just such an opportunity for two decades, but when it finally arrived, it was a complete whirlwind. In six days, I had gone from relative unknown to star. It was comparable to what might have happened if, years later, I had ignored Jack Moran's guffaw, entered that initial Twin Cities Marathon, and not only beaten Alex Ratelle but set a world record.

## Ninth Attempt: Going Galloway, Edmonton, Alberta—1996

I waited more than three months before attempting my next marathon. It was the Capitol City Marathon in Edmonton, Alberta—an event with slightly fewer than one thousand participants. I was invited by the folks at the Running Room, whose Kelowna store sponsored the Okanagan Marathon, and having never been to Alberta before, I took advantage of the opportunity to check it out.

Edmonton is a tidy city in the northern plains, far enough east of the Rockies that mountains aren't visible on the horizon, even on the clearest of days. The course was rolling but not too difficult—definitely one on which it was possible to run a fast time. The elevation, though, was a bit of a challenge: roughly 2,200 feet above sea level, which is enough to slow a three-hour marathoner down by about two minutes.

Having run poor performances in my last two marathons, I had decided not to take this one seriously. Of course, there was always the chance that I might get started in the race and discover I was having a good day. Hope, as they say, springs eternal. My real problem was that I was emotionally worn out. This was my ninth marathon in a little more than 18 months, and like all but one of the others, it had required a significant amount of travel.

My duties included radio, TV, and newspaper interviews. In the process, I met one of the other speakers, Jeff Galloway, who was advocating a new approach to marathoning that would soon come to bear his name. Rather than running the entire distance nonstop, he urged, try taking short walk breaks once per mile. Jeff himself has done this and can cite some very fast marathoners who have done the same, posting times much faster than I needed.

I had always taken walk breaks on long training runs but never in races, except by necessity. Jeff suggested that as long as I wasn't making a serious attempt at the record, I might try his technique, planning a 10- to 20-second walk break each mile.

Race day dawned cool, but it was August, and by the time we finished it was probably in the low 80s. Even though I had told the race director I wasn't running for the record, he seeded me with the elites, probably hoping to inspire me to change my mind. I started comfortably and settled into a pace that was about one second per mile faster than my target world-record pace. As usual, I quickly hooked up with younger runners going at about my pace. One recognized me from the clinic. He asked what pace I needed for the record, and our entire group sped up from 6:55s to 6:48s.

At mile seven, I decided to try one of Jeff's walk breaks. My companions ran on ahead, while I walked briskly but comfortably for about 30 or 40 paces, testing to see whether the rest would allow me to go faster when I returned to running. It appeared to work and I caught my companions well before mile eight and then moved ahead, telling them I would see them again when I took my next break.

We continued this way until mile 21, at which point my companions fell off pace. But while I was running comfortably, the walk breaks were taking a toll in time, and the record wasn't within striking range.

I finished in 3:09:04. It was still well slower than anything I had done last year, but at least I was continuing to move in the right direction. Galloway's method, I decided, is a good way to run a marathon without overexerting yourself but not the way to get your best possible time. There's a reason you never see anyone do it in the Olympics.

## Hair-Raising Stuff: England—Circa 1970

*"Hey John, I was reading in the* News of the World *that there's an excellent remedy for falling hair,"* our principal comedian was telling me.

*I took the bait and asked what it was.*

*"You catch it in a paper bag."*

• • •

For me, it was no laughing matter. I was lead tenor in a touring revue, and everyone knew I was concerned about losing my leading-male looks by getting thinner on top. So far, nobody but me could actually see a difference. But each morning, studying my comb, I could see the trend. So when our piano accompanist told me of a cure recommended by an aging friend, he had my attention.

The friend had known of a soldier in the Boer War in South Africa who had recounted a story about hair loss. It was an era when horses were still used to pull field artillery, and the shafts of the caissons would chafe the horses' flanks, giving them painful sores where all of the hair had been abraded off. To treat this and get the horses back into action as soon as possible, the artillerymen concocted a salve of gunpowder and lard. A side effect of the treatment was that the hair grew back quickly and strongly, and some of the older soldiers figured that what worked for horses ought to work for people. According to the pianist's friend, it had been quite successful.

Two other members of the revue were also balding, so I volunteered to acquire the ingredients to make enough gunpowder pomade to serve us all.

The lard was easy. I went to a butcher's shop and bought a pound of suet. Then I headed for a sporting goods store specializing in shotguns and other hunting goods. In Great Britain the acquisition of guns requires a license, and the rules are strict. I asked the proprietor if I might buy some gunpowder, just a small amount, and he told me that unless I had a business license for making ammunition, there was no way he could sell it to me.

I explained that I didn't want to shoot anyone and that I only wanted a small amount, but he wouldn't budge. Nor would he sell me cartridges from which I could remove the bullet and extract the powder, even when I told him why I wanted the gunpowder. Even though he had heard of the gunpowder/lard hair restorer and had been told it was quite effective, he still held firm. The law was the law, and he just couldn't do it. He, of course, had a shock of thick curly hair that would never need help.

As I was starting to leave, he glanced around the store, which was empty of other customers. "You know," he said, "you can buy the ingredients at any drugstore." He then reminded me that gunpowder is made of saltpeter, charcoal, and sulfur. "Just don't tell them I sent you."

I thanked him and resumed my quest at the first drugstore I saw, a block down the street.

In England, the pharmacist usually sits in an anteroom off the main shop, where he can work uninterrupted. At the moment, however, he was at the sales counter, standing in for his assistant, who was out to lunch. I might have been better off waiting for the assistant's return. The pharmacist smiled ruefully at my request. "You're going to make gunpowder, aren't you?"

I admitted I was and explained about the lard and the Boer War horses. If the pharmacist had heard the story before, he gave no sign. "I'm sorry," he said. "It is illegal for me to dispense these ingredients, and you will not find any respectable chemist who will do it. But"—he paused—"there is nothing to stop you from buying each ingredient separately from three different sources."

I thanked him and bought a pound of sulfur. As I was leaving the store, he stopped me.

"Are you planning on mixing it with a mortar and pestle?"

I hadn't thought much about it, but that seemed reasonable, presuming that I could locate such instruments.

"Go easy on the grinding," he said.

• • •

My landlady was kindly and tolerant, accustomed to the idiosyncrasies of the actors. She even had a mortar and pestle. She had only one request. "Please don't blow us all up."

Needless to say, I had never made gunpowder before. I was a bit vague about the ingredient ratios but figured I couldn't go too far wrong, especially since I wasn't trying to make munitions. I started out with the saltpeter, which was a lumpy powder that tended to make irritating little clots. Then I set to work on the charcoal. The sulfur was already nicely powdered. Meanwhile, I had rendered the suet to lard in a frying pan.

In retrospect, the combination of stove flame and homemade gunpowder in a small room might not have been the most intelligent thing I had ever done, but I got away with it. When the lard cooled, I mixed all of the ingredients in a chipped ceramic bowl.

Then, finally, I was ready to do something to arrest my thinning hair. At the bathroom basin I washed and dried my hair and proceeded to massage the mixture into my scalp. The application was uncomfortably gritty, but biting the bullet, as it were, I continued until I had covered all of the areas of concern. Then I combed my sticky locks and went to clean up the mess I had made in my landlady's kitchen.

A parting glance in the mirror showed my greasy head shining in the light. I looked as though I could stand in a full gale without a single hair being blown out of place.

By the time I had cleaned the kitchen it was suppertime. Then I was off to the theater. My landlady gave me a couple of small jars into which I meted out enough of the magic hair cream for my friends. As I rose from the dining table, however, I became acutely aware that there is a problem with a hair ointment made, in part, of sulfur.

"Can you smell that?" I asked my landlady. I myself was on the verge of being overpowered, but I was close to the source, so maybe nobody else would notice. I had some close scenes with other actors in the upcoming show. Would the scent be obvious?

"Yes," my landlady said.

Still, I entered the stage door under the illusion that I might somehow be aromatically inoffensive. It wasn't until my fellow actors greeted me that I remembered that the aroma wasn't the only thing that had changed.

"I see you got a haircut," someone said.

"What have you done to your head?"

"A new hairstyle, eh?"

Not a "phew" yet, though, so maybe I was in luck. I delivered the jars to two other needy actors who were delighted to know I was already testing it. It was too late for them to do the same tonight, but they would start straight-away in the morning. And yes, they could notice the smell but assured me that they weren't offended.

"It's a bit like a smelly fart," the balder of the two said. "But who cares, as long as it works?"

I now realize that bald spots from chafing aren't the same as bald spots from aging. Those Boer War horses would have started growing hair the moment the chafing was eliminated. I have no idea whether the gunpowder helped.

Each day, the smell of sulfur was becoming more objectionable, and the "goupilard," as we came to call it, was uncomfortably abrasive. We had hoped to market it and make a fortune. Instead we were getting sore scalps.

When I quit, it took a week of daily washing for my scalp to begin smelling of shampoo rather than sulfur. Even then, I had to live with the reek of sulfur in my pillow. The smell would greet me each night and then reimpregnate my hair as I slept, until I insisted that my landlady change the pillowslip more frequently. Then each pillowslip would absorb some of the stink out of the underlying pillow, in a slow process I thought would never end.

I wasn't the only one who found it hard to rid himself of the last traces of sulfur. Some of the women of the company tried to help by lending us highly scented shampoos. Each evening they would diligently sniff our heads to see whether that day's shampoo was more successful than the one before.

"No luck," one would say. "This one still stinks like the old tomcat my mum had put down last year."

"And this one reminds me of those grotty toilets in Newcastle railway station."

The most sensitive noses were still picking up hints of sulfur when we moved to the next town, a full two weeks after we had abandoned our growth therapy. Our comedian threatened to write a sketch about us, but thankfully it never materialized, and goupilard disappeared into the pantheon of useless ways to ward off the signs of aging.

## CHAPTER 15

# Last Chances

## From Don Juan to Country Don: England and Minnesota—1974–75

*Sweet Charity* was a smash hit. I got a great write-up and played more than four hundred performances in 18 months. It later became a movie, with Ricardo Montalban as Vittorio, Shirley MacLaine as Charity, and John McMartin and Sammy Davis Jr. That success led to others, so many that they are hard to remember because I never thought to keep an acting diary as detailed as the running logs I would later employ.

Then one day, I had a surprise visitor. It was 1974, and I was playing three minor roles in a musical called *Billy* when a middle-aged gentleman knocked on my dressing-room door. "Hi, John," he said. He seemed to think I should know him.

Fans will sometimes talk to you that way, but none should have been able to get to my dressing room.

"You don't recognize me, do you?" he said, seeming to be enjoying the moment. He had a full beard, neatly trimmed, and a peaked kangatype hat, none of which rang any bells. His accent was American.

"Fulton?" I asked. Was this my stage and oven-cleaning companion from Indiana University? "Fulton Gallagher?"

I had not seen him since 1963, but we had kept in touch via letters and Christmas cards. After finishing his PhD, he had wound up in academe, at a place called Bemidji State University, where he had risen to head the department of music.

He had not written to tell me he was coming, he now told me, because the trip had been arranged on short notice by a friend who had come into possession of a pair of free tickets and wanted a companion for a quick trip. What a far cry from decades before, when my own transatlantic journeys had required 10 days' travel, each way!

"How are you doing?" Fulton asked. It was a pretty ordinary question, and most people would have given a fairly standard answer. *Billy* was a classy production whose cast was loaded with people who would later have prominent careers, the type of thing that might have paved my own way to film stardom. I had even managed, a few years earlier, to fit in some opera, singing the male lead in *Lucia di Lammermoor* at an opera festival in Waterford, Ireland. To all appearances, I was doing well.

But the words that escaped my lips were ones that only Anne had heard before. "I'm miserable," I heard myself say. "Don't get me wrong. I'm glad I came here, glad I stayed. But I'm ready for a change. And the commute is killing me."

Of course, the commute was my own choice. I could have avoided it by living in London. But my years in America had made me fond of open spaces. Anne and I had bought a Georgian-era home in Wantage, a charming town on the edge of the Cotswolds. I had remodeled it myself, serving as my own architect, general contractor, and interior decorator. Much of what I did was exotic, and Anne was sometimes convinced it would never work, but it always did.

I have always liked artistic diversity, and working on the home had given me a new venue in which to vent the restlessness that always set in when I stayed too long in one place. In running, I've competed at every distance from the 200 meters to the marathon. There are people who devote their entire careers—musical or athletic—to a single domain, but that would never have been me. But renovating the house had come at a price. Our home in Wantage, Oxfordshire, was 75 miles from London.

"I'm commuting a thousand miles a week," I told Fulton. Between the train and the subway and driving to and from the station, it took three hours each way. "Why don't you offer me a job?"

It was one of those remarks said in jest but not entirely meant that way. And amazingly, it turned out to be why Fulton was here. He called Anne, and that night the three of us and his friend met after the evening show. I had no solos in *Billy*, and since he wanted to hear me sing, we went to a place with the amusingly cross-cultural name of Yoshi's Old Vienna Restaurant, one of my favorite haunts when I was in plays that didn't give me as much singing as I wanted. I had learned some German operetta and would sometimes sing (quite literally) for my dinner. This time, Fulton and the others were fed as well, while I sang not only songs from German operettas but anything else that seemed like fun.

• • •

A few months later, Fulton and his wife visited us in Wantage. He had persuaded his university in Minnesota to create an artist-in-residence program and wanted me as the first artist. It was a one-year appointment with flexible starting and ending dates, something like a sabbatical from which I could then return to full-time stage. It sounded idyllic. Anne asked about teaching options. She meant high school, but Fulton did her one better and came through with a graduate assistantship at the university, teaching freshman English. We also peppered him with questions about the climate, which had an intimidating reputation. Like any good Minnesotan, he lied by saying, "It's not really all that bad," then converted that to truth by adding, "You get used to it." You really do, though it would take us two winters to believe it.

• • •

In British theater, when an actor signs for a play, it's almost always for the run of the production, however extended that might be. But because I wasn't in a leading role and because the producers of *Billy* had come to me, rather than my going to them, I'd had the bargaining clout to insist on an escape clause. I wound up with dual reason to exercise it.

At about the time Fulton was recruiting me for Bemidji State, I was offered a role in a Royal Shakespeare Company production of *Sherlock Holmes* that would spend several months touring in the United States. I could use it as a stepping-stone to Bemidji by moving to Minnesota when *Sherlock Holmes* completed its run.

The Royal Shakespeare Company vies with the National Theatre as England's finest company. Fulton was thrilled at being able to tell the folks in Minnesota that he had recruited a Royal Shakespeare Company performer, so we were decided. Anne would take the teaching position in Bemidji; I would do *Sherlock Holmes* and then join the family in the frigid north woods. My role in the play (which was written in 1897 by none other than Sir Arthur Conan Doyle himself) was Sir Edward Leighton, who employs Holmes to retrieve from a Miss Faulkner letters that could damage the reputation of a noble English family. I also understudied the lead role of Sherlock. I had once played the detective in a television commercial for Brooke Bond Tea. The rehearsals were exacting and meticulous, but also fun.

Then at last we were off to America, first for six weeks in the Kennedy Center in Washington, DC, and then for three months on Broadway, at the Broadhurst Theater. It was a spectacular way to make what would prove to be my exit from major league theater. I had done a great deal of touring in my life but never in such fine company or such wonderful venues. In Washington, we were treated like royalty. In New York, we were a smash hit, and our set designers won a Tony Award.

•   •   •

Anne and the family spent Christmas with me in New York, then two months later I joined them in Minnesota, just in time for the euphemistically termed "spring" quarter. (In Minnesota, there is no true spring. Rather, there are four seasons in rapid succession: winter, mud, mosquitoes, and heat.) Anne was already established, teaching freshman literature and composition. Now it was my turn. Virtually overnight, it seemed, we had both become academics. One advantage of arriving in March was that the truly deep cold of midwinter was well gone, although it was still the coldest climate I had ever experienced. But I soon came to love it. By the time, a few years later, I actually frostbit a certain delicate portion of the male anatomy, I had long been a dedicated Minnesotan.

## One Final Preparation: McMinnville—1996

My last three marathons had been getting better, but I was still seven minutes and 49 seconds shy of the world record. I needed a whopping 18 seconds per mile—roughly equivalent to the difference between the 41:55 10K that had set Jack Moran to guffawing all those years ago and the sub-40:00 I had needed to compete with Alex Ratelle. But that had been comparatively easy because I had been a beginner, and beginners take a while to find their true potential. Worse, each passing month was making the goal more difficult. By the time I was 72, the WAVA tables bleakly told me that running a 3:00 marathon would be equivalent to running a 2:55:53 at age 70: more than four minutes faster than the goal that had eluded me in Houston, Valencia, London, Kelowna, Clackamas, and Grandma's. Not good. Worse, my PR was a 2:52:38 run at age 62. Forget the sub-3:00; to beat that 3:01:14 record at age 71-plus, I was going to need the equivalent of a 62-year-old's 2:43. I wasn't just going to need to beat the aging curve; I was going to have to shatter it.

I was going to have to run the race of my life.

I was also going to need some help. So I called up Hal Goforth, an exercise physiologist who worked in San Diego for the Navy, helping determine optimum training regimens for the Navy's equivalent of boot camp. He also coached the Navy's competitive runners, who travel to national meets to compete against the Air Force, Army, and Marines.

I had known Hal for some time as a runner and a fine age-group performer, and I knew that if there was anyone with an idea of how to whip a 71-1/2-year-old body into peak shape, it would be him. I also knew he would work me hard. His personal regimen was intense, and people who trained with him tended to improve.

We developed a three-month program, targeted on the cool weather of fall: my last serious chance at the record before turning 72 and most likely my last chance at it, ever. By e-mail, he sent me a customized program of long, intermediate, and short runs not all that different from what I had been doing. The main difference was that Hal was a fan of tempo runs. On the days when I ran long (up to 20 miles), I continued to go slowly, and on the days when I ran short, I continued to do fast intervals on the track. But on the intermediate days, when I was running 10 to 15 miles, he had me incorporate brisk segments at a pace only 15 or 20 seconds per mile slower than my all-out racing pace for the same distance—starting at three miles and gradually building up to eight. I had never done much of that type of workout before, and they seemed intimidating. But Hal assured me this is what the young elites did, so I set about following his regimen as meticulously as possible. If I still didn't make my goal, it wasn't going to be for wimping out in training.

## Master's Degree: Bemidji State University—1975

My duties at Bemidji State were a mix of performing and teaching. I had enjoyed the teaching I had done at Indiana University and had continued teaching off and on in England but wasn't sure it qualified me to work at the university level. Fulton, though, convinced me that it was just the old impostor syndrome in a new setting. "You'll be one of the best voice teachers the university ever had," he assured me, and I found myself attacking academe with the same enthusiasm I would soon bring to running.

By the end of the first quarter, I knew I wanted more than a visiting position. There was just one minor hitch: artist-in-residence programs are different from standard teaching ones because they allow real-world experience to substitute for the college degree that is nearly universally required of traditional professors. I could make a temporary switch to a position as an "instructor," but that was a low-level position from which there could be no promotion without the degree. So I set about filling in the gaps from my days at Indiana—joining my students in classes like philosophy and English, whatever was needed to cobble the pieces of my life and education together into a formal degree. I even took a course in sailing to meet a physical education requirement.

Whether or not Fulton was right about the "best teacher" bit, I soon discovered that I was good at it and that I enjoyed giving eager young performers the things so many others had given me. From the start, I was involved in every aspect of their work: teaching voice, directing performances, and designing and putting on productions. Running coaches now tell me the same thing: there is no greater thrill than showing others how to do something difficult, convincing them they really can do it, and greeting them when it's over. Not that there isn't any anxiety. I know a running coach who always has two speeches prepared: one that begins, "I knew you could do it!" and another, which he calls his "damage-control" speech. Rarely, though, do you have to give the latter. And unlike a running coach, I often got to perform with my students in recital—adding a duet to their repertoire and watching my presence on stage with them fill them with confidence and quiet their nerves.

• • •

Performing was also part of my job, but it was very different from commercial theater. Even at the height of my commercial career, I had felt compelled to take almost every job that came my way. I would turn things down only if I thought I could do something better. In addition, shows could run for quite a while. Learning a new role is fun and artistically challenging. Repeating the same performance dozens or hundreds of times is at best craft and at worst, work. The running equivalent might be doing a 10K every week on the same course. Once you've got it mastered, a lot of the pleasure goes out of it.

All performers also have things they want to do but which nobody will ever pay for. Bemidji was a long way from the Kennedy Center and the London stage, but I could branch out as far as I liked. I even put together recitals of Spanish, French, and Italian art songs for which there couldn't possibly have been a commercial market.

By the time I had completed my undergraduate degree, I knew that this was the place where I would finish my career, working with students and creating my own productions. And in 1980, when jogging and then racing began to infuse my life, the mind-set of the runner began to infuse my music. I never regretted my glory days in London—my life would have been much diminished without them—but now I was performing on my terms, not someone else's.

•   •   •

When I finished my undergraduate degree, I could have gone through commencement exercises with my students, but I declined that honor. Instead, I set to work on my master's degree. For that, you need a thesis.

I had long ago noticed that if you are performing classical "art" songs, most people presume you will be singing in a language they don't understand. It's one of the reasons there is a limited audience for such music. But there is actually a rich literature of English and American art songs, overlooked by years of the snobbish presumption that if it's not in French, Italian, or German, it's not really "art." For my thesis, I set to work uncovering these songs and presenting them in recital. I quickly discovered that my students also enjoyed singing in their native tongue, so that rather than being a purely academic exercise, my thesis helped resurrect this material for a whole generation of Midwestern singers.

On stage, I was now too old for leading-man roles but perfect for some of the theater's more interesting characters. Remembering my days teaching ʃs to my Pakistani friend, I took a role with a community theater production of *My Fair Lady* as Henry Higgins—the crotchety British linguist who teaches upper-crust British diction to a young cockney woman. During my stay in New York City, I had seen a play called *Brief Lives*, based on the work of 17th-century writer John Aubrey. Many of the play's character sketches reflected my lifelong fascination with aging, so I acquired the rights to perform materials from it and began combining them with other pieces that would become a one-man show on aging.

Had I stayed with the Royal Shakespeare Company and productions like *Billy*, I might well have gone on to a life of even greater success on the stage or film. I sometimes wonder what might have happened had I tried it, but it's merely an academic curiosity. At Bemidji State, I no longer felt compelled to take any old acting job just to pay the bills. I could perform what I wanted and only what I wanted, expressing myself artistically better than ever before.

By the time I had been there five years, I had found an entirely new form of self-expression as a runner.

## Summit Street: Minneapolis, Minnesota—1996

*Singing the national anthem at races is immensely important to me. It's a way to combine the two passions that I have pursued throughout my life, while also paying tribute to the country that took me in, assisted my training, and gave me citizenship. The only drawback, minor compared to the benefits, is that the need to warm up my voice in private draws me away from the prerace company of my fellow runners. And thus, in the minutes before the Twin Cities Marathon, I found myself oddly alone, even as thousands of other runners gathered for the start.*

• • •

I never quite built up to the eight-mile tempo runs recommended by Hal Goforth because I wanted to race a month earlier than his 13-week program permitted. Specifically, I wanted a familiar course with fond memories and nearby family: the Twin Cities Marathon, traditionally the first weekend of October.

Even though I had truncated Hal's program, I felt I was as well prepared as I ever would be. The tempo runs (I had gotten up to six-milers) had given me substantially more speed work than ever before in my life, and I was also racing and logging as much mileage as I dared. In the previous 12 weeks, I had run more than 700 miles. My Galloway-style race in Edmonton might not have given me a great time, but it hadn't tired me, and I had recovered quickly and raced 10 more times at distances from 800 to 10,000 meters, with a three-weekend sequence of four races: a 39:40 10K; a double-header 39:40 10K and 32:10 8K on back-to-back days; and a 32:07 5-miler. None were quite all-out efforts, and each was faster than the one before. Some people perform better if they race less frequently, but I've always used races as part of my training.

Every year for nearly a decade, I had been invited to come to the Twin Cities Marathon at the race's expense, and I had now run the route four times. And while it was a point-to-point course, it was very slightly uphill, and its start and finish were (just barely) close enough together to qualify for an official record. It was also a staggeringly beautiful course. When Jack Moran, still its race director and now a man with whom I was on perfectly friendly terms, created it, he billed it "The World's Most Beautiful Urban Marathon." On a perfect autumn day, with crisp skies and maple leaves edging toward peak color, it more than lives up to his claim. Running from downtown Minneapolis to the state capitol, it spends most of its distance on boulevards and parkways, with lakes, a high crossing over the Mississippi River, and a long final straightaway aiming right at the capitol dome.

• • •

*One advantage of having done the race so many times before was that I had found a private place to warm up my voice, a church not far from the building where the elite runners warm up (and have access to uncrowded elite-only bathrooms!). Even if there were people there preparing for the morning service (and usually there were not), warming up my voice in front of them was far less disconcerting than doing so in the elite-runners' building. After all, the church's own choir would soon be doing the same. In my own private haven, I limbered up body and voice . . . and waited.*

• • •

A week before the marathon, Anne and I stayed in a hotel near the Portland, Oregon, airport. We had booked a noon flight, so the next morning, six days before the marathon, I took my last long run—16 miles in two hours flat: a 7:30 pace. For the first time that year, I felt the confidence I had felt going into my attempts at the record the year before. Barring yet another round of bad luck, I would run well. Whether it would be well enough remained to be seen.

Part of the price of accepting the marathon's offer of free travel was that my attempt at the record would be part of the prerace publicity. The next day, after a pleasant evening with Pamela and her family, I did an interview with a reporter from the *Minneapolis Star Tribune,* and then a photographer took me for a photo shoot, running with my son John around one of the city's many lakes. Happily, when the article was printed, it talked mostly about me as a 71-year-old racer and downplayed my hope for the record. I was good enough at putting too much pressure on myself; I certainly didn't need more from the media.

My final long run in Portland had been a glycogen-depletion run as part of a carbohydrate depletion/rebound program that, if timed correctly, might give me a slight boost late in the race. The theory is that by depleting your glycogen reserves with a long run and then holding them down for three days by eating a very low-carbohydrate diet (while continuing to do short runs to burn off whatever carbohydrates do get into your system), you make the body so starved for carbohydrates that when you finally start eating them again, it overshoots and stores more than normal. You then try to do the marathon right at the peak of the rebound.

The downside is that by the third day of the depletion, you can barely run. I had run only five miles on my photo shoot, but I woke the following morning feeling horribly tired. That day, I was supposed to do the same distance, with the second and fourth miles at a brisk, tempoish pace. I ran the warm-up, kicked up the speed . . . and was so wiped out 800 meters into the first tempo mile that I had to stop, gasping for breath. I jogged a bit and managed to complete my run but with four 800-meter tempo intervals, rather than the planned miles.

I had done the depletion/rebound program before and knew it wasn't a confidence booster. Here I was, less than 96 hours from my planned shot at the world marathon record, and I could barely run around the block. But at least I knew the solution. I wasn't supposed to start the rebound until dinner, but the heck with that. I went back to Pamela's and ate six slices of toast, five slices of bacon, and three eggs. I lathered the toast with black-current jam and ladled two teaspoons of sugar into each of three cups of tea. Then I took a nap. With a few more good breakfasts and lunches and a couple of spaghetti dinners, I was determined to be ready to go come race day.

• • •

As usual for Minneapolis in October, it was cool at the start, and I had to rub my arms and legs to keep them warm. But there were no shivers in my voice during the anthem, and I held the final note for a long, steady moment before finishing.

I then hurried to the starting line, where I hunched between the young elites, trying to stay warm.

Then we were off. Starting so far forward usually draws me out fast, and this morning was no exception. Even though runners were streaming by me in the first mile, I hit the one-mile mark in 6:39—faster than ideal, but for once I didn't worry about it. With most of the fast runners ahead now and fewer passing me, I was slower in the second mile, completing it in 6:58. Mile three went up a slight rise and was slower yet, a 7:08, and for what might have been the first time in my racing career, I was actually behind my target pace early in a race. I eased forward, looking for a 6:45.

Meanwhile, I was passing a steady parade of Minneapolis landmarks. First was the Guthrie Theater, one of Minnesota's most famous. Then came the Walker Art Center, Lake of the Isles, Lake Calhoun, and Lake Harriet, all with charming residential neighborhoods where spectators were out in force. Through these, my pace continued to fluctuate, partly in response to the encouraging crowds, partly due to minor irregularities in the terrain: 7:08, 6:42, 6:48. Eventually I found a comfortable groove and began engaging other runners in conversation. One fellow from New York was bubbling with delight over this lovely course. His name was Alan and he was 47, with thick, dark, wavy hair. He was perhaps two inches shorter than me but 20 pounds heavier, with bodybuilder muscles. He had done a dozen marathons in as many states (eventually he hoped to hit all 50) and thought this was by far the most scenic he had ever encountered.

We ran together along the shore of Lake Harriet, where in previous years my family had waited to cheer me along. This year, they were farther down the course, somewhere between mile seven and mile eight.

"You look familiar," Alan said. "What do you do for a living?"

That's never an easy question, but I gave him a brief synopsis—singer, actor, teacher, now retired.

"That's it," he said. "You sang the 'Star-Spangled Banner,' didn't you? What a great job—not like all those pop singers who destroy the melody with too much ornamentation."

I shared the same sentiment, believing that the anthem was best sung straight rather than the way so many people do it, with embellishments that can make it nearly unrecognizable. But I was surprised at his use of the technical term "ornamentation" until he continued: "I teach music and band in a high school in upstate New York. You must have retired awfully early, or you're an awfully young-looking 60."

I can never let that one pass. "I'm nearly 72," I said, feeling the corners of my mouth pull back in a smile.

By now, we had cleared the last of the lakes and were running toward the dawn on a wide boulevard along Minnehaha Creek, named for Hiawatha's wife in Longfellow's famous poem. Alan was afraid he was slowing me down, but so far, we were right on pace, and it was good to have company. The sun was a bright ball, still low to the horizon, slanting through huge trees, slowly shedding their burden of autumn fire and gold. Now and then, a falling leaf would caress me. It was a perfect running moment, one of the finest I'd had since the Clackamas Canyon Marathon, 16 months before. As at that race, I felt how wonderful life was and how splendid it was to be clicking off the miles in good company, with the cares and concerns of everyday life momentarily rendered insignificant. We can never know how fast we will be in future races or even the number of them fate has in store, but I can say with certainty that as long as the body permits, I will continue to seek these moments, even as my pace drops from 6:45s to 7:00s, to 8:00s, and—if I live long enough—to 9:00s and slower.

A water station loomed and I edged to the side of the road to grab a cup on the run, being extremely careful not to lose everything by again being shoved or tripped. It is difficult to drink on the run, but I had decided that this time I wouldn't take even the briefest of walk breaks. Alan wasn't as skilled at this as I was, and he fell slightly back. I slowed, waiting for him (giving up the time I had gained by running through the aid station), and moments later he was again with me. Briefly, I wondered whether I actually was letting him hold me back, but we went through mile 12 at another 6:48, still well ahead of pace. But a mile later, the pace had slowed to 6:52. Just as I wondered what to say, Alan complained of a tight calf and stopped to stretch. We promised to look for each other at the finish, but I never did see him.

Unfortunately, I wasn't going any faster. Mile 14 was a 6:58; mile 15 was a 7:06. I was alarmed, though mile 15 had included a significant upgrade with a tight corner. Still, it was time to concentrate on maintaining pace. Picking up the tempo, I ran 6:48 for the next mile, watching my heart rate monitor to see whether I might be overdoing it. Happily, it registered 148 beats per minute, exactly what it had been for most of the race. I had given up 14 seconds on the hill, but now I had gotten half of them back. The next two miles were faster yet: a pair of 6:43s, and my heart rate had risen only to 151.

With 8.2 miles to go, I had only a minute in the bank on world-record pace, but oddly, I wasn't worried. So many times before, I had hit mile 18 with a lot more cushion than that, only to lose it in the final miles. But this time I felt far more confident than that narrow window would seem to have warranted. Sixty seconds: I could lose that in a single cramping calf, a fall, dehydration—or any of a number of ways I had not previously experienced. But maybe those slow three miles at the start had been the magic formula, because right now I felt as though I could keep going, if not forever, at least as long as necessary.

I was in the zone and knew it. I relaxed my mind and body, concentrating (to the extent that is compatible with relaxation) on retaining the rhythm of the past 18 miles and letting that rhythm—not me, not the watch, not time in the bank—be the force that carried me to whatever the result might be.

I tried to make my mind blank, to be an animal, not a calculator. But instead, it wandered.

With so many decades of living behind me, there are a lot of places for it to wander, but one where it frequently goes, especially when I've sung the national anthem earlier in the day, is to the linkages between my running and singing careers. Some are obvious: the intense effort I've brought to each; the wondrous sensation when the pieces come together and everything goes right; the ease with which I can replay those intensely lived moments, years afterward. But some links are more subtle. Now my thoughts drifted to a time when I deliberately applied sports-training methods to singing.

It was when I was singing in the Catskills. I had long before noted that most of the great tenors of opera had large . . . girths. Among the cognoscenti, in fact, it was generally accepted that that gives a larger . . . foundation . . . to the highest notes. Vocally, what I most cherished were the high notes. What I most wanted was to go higher still. But by tenor standards, I was always rather scrawny. Probably, the link that stirred up this long-ago memory was Alan, with his New York origins, knowledgeable talk of music, and weightlifter physique. In the Catskills, I had decided to do something about bulking up, but not wanting to get fat, I turned to weightlifting. I asked a local bodybuilder to give me a workout schedule and threw myself into it wholeheartedly: every day would find me in the gym, working whatever muscle group I could think of. I was particularly fond of sit-ups, hoping that by strengthening the abdominals, some of the benefit would spill over to the diaphragm. I had also been advised to eat a high-protein diet, so I bought a protein supplement. Twice a day, I mixed it in a blender with milk, adding three raw eggs just for good measure. Today I would probably have to run five or six miles to burn off each glass of this concoction, but I was younger then, with a more active metabolism.

On top of this, my bodybuilding friends encouraged me to eat my normal meals. The result was a sensation quite different from running the middle miles of a marathon with the body on cruise control. I did not feel light on my feet; I felt bloated after every drink, fat and sluggish all the rest of the time. Worse, I developed perpetual flatulence. On stage, I tried not to grimace as I held it in, but in the gym everyone seemed to be in the same state and often, when someone pushed a big weight skyward you could hear, above the clank of the iron, a distinct rumble. But the most embarrassing exercise was the squat, where containment was impossible and each repetition was backed by the most indiscreet accompaniments. Runners like to joke that such things speed you up via jet propulsion. In the weight room, a distinct fug hung in the atmosphere whenever more than a few of us were present.

Throughout this process, I became enamored of mirrors. Whenever I saw one, I would stop and flex my biceps to see how much it might have grown. When I started my exercise-and-protein regimen, my biceps measured 13 3/4 inches. Two months later, they measured all of fourteen inches. I was even gaining a little weight, though not a lot. (There is obviously a metabolic reason why I have maintained a fine, lean racing weight throughout my running career despite years of extravagant carboloading dinners.) But my belly hurt all the time, and I was afraid Anne would start wearing nose plugs and earplugs at night so she didn't have to smell or hear me.

But the final test lay in the singing. I practiced and practiced, but despite all the work and discomfort, my high notes did not sound any more brilliant, nor could I sustain a healthy high C any better than before. My trainer insisted that I would eventually get used to my new diet, but that it would take "a good long while." Meanwhile, I was tooting a bit on too many of those not-really-improved high notes. I gave up the supplements, which were rather pricey, anyway, but continued to lift weights for several years, eventually gaining 10 pounds by the time I moved back to London.

Now, of course, I had long ago given up all of my bodybuilding gains. Who wants to carry big pecs and biceps around for 26 miles? The muscles I wanted now were in my legs.

• • •

The trouble with letting your mind wander is that you slow down. Mile 19 passed at a 6:58, and I was down to less than a minute in the time bank, with Summit Hill yet ahead. First, though, the course crossed the Mississippi River, turned south to parallel it, and went through the archway of the theatrical castle that still marked the dreaded 20-mile "wall," just as it had the first time I had run the course, a decade before. I glided through the portal, grabbed another drink without breaking stride, and checked my pace: 6:57. No problem. With 6.2 miles to go, I could afford 7:04s.

Mile 21 came and went, also at a 6:57, and then mile 22 brought a 7:10. But that was understandable because the course had dipped beneath a bridge and then climbed steeply back out of the underpass. Upgrades always take away more time than you gain from the downgrade, so I hadn't really slowed down. I was now a mere 40 seconds ahead of record pace, but the end was getting closer and I could afford 7:05s for the final 4.2 miles, at least if I kicked a bit in the last few yards. More important, I still felt strong.

We were now at Summit Avenue, still in Minneapolis but heading for St. Paul. Four miles away, straight ahead, lay the state capitol and the end of my quest, one way or another. I didn't have much time to waste, but I was still ahead of pace and running better for this late in the race than in any of my other world-record attempts. If I couldn't do it this time, I probably never could.

In its early years, the race followed a different route to Summit Avenue, winding through a residential neighborhood, up and over a significant hill. But that route had been discarded in favor of a straight-line finish on Summit. It was simpler, more direct, and—all important for me now—it dodged most of the hill. Instead, the course ran very gradually uphill until mile 25 1/2. It was a long upgrade but not really a big one, and the finish was a nice little downgrade.

Richard had come down from Wisconsin to watch, and he and John were waiting at mile 23, where they would run with me toward the top of that long, slow hill. They appeared right on schedule, one on each side, just as I had clocked a 6:53. I could now afford 7:08s for the final 3.2 miles.

I later learned that they had agreed not to ask how I felt and to tell me, no matter what, that I was "right on target," "looking good," and "going to do it." They ran with me a bit, trying to whip up crowd support, and then dropped off because none of us were quite sure of the rules about pacers.

Mile 24 was a 6:58 despite the upgrade. All I needed now were a pair of 7:12s and I had it in the bag. Mile 25 was slow—something on the wrong side of 7:20—because the hill got steeper, but a half mile later, I was over the crest and into the downgrade, where all I needed was to kick it in—and that was easy because I had done my training right and was feeling on top of the world. I started pushing even before the crest, speeding up to hit the final 1.2 miles at what a bit of math later told me was a 6:47 pace—my third-fastest split of the entire race.

And then, amazingly, the record was mine. It had taken 10 attempts in 21 months, but I had run 3:00:58, beating the old mark by 16 seconds. Two months before my 72nd birthday, I had indeed run the finest race of my life.

• • •

Despite the low-key prerace coverage in the newspaper, the press knew what I had been attempting, and my graying hair, now significantly thin on top, made me easy to spot. "Are you going to Disneyland to celebrate?" a television reporter asked.

"No," I laughed. "A pint of Summit Ale will suffice." It wasn't until later that I realized that this excellent brew was named for the avenue I had just run.

The best media coverage came from the sports section of the *Minneapolis Star Tribune*:

> A 71-year-old Briton belted out the national anthem (the American one) before Sunday's Twin Cities Marathon, but it was not his high note for the day. . . (He) waltzed to a world age-group record with a time of 3 hours, 58 seconds. . . 'Hey, I'm nearly 72,' he said after finishing 235th among a field of 7,058.

It might be the best review I've ever received.

## CHAPTER 16

# What's Next?

## Racing From *Riven*: San Francisco—February 1997

I have never fully retired from performing. Today's performances largely take the form of renditions of the national anthem (or perhaps "Danny Boy" or "When Irish Eyes are Smiling" for St. Patrick's Day races), but when Anne and I again moved to Oregon, I wasted no time hunting up an agent. Mostly, I did modeling—a photo shoot for Mercedes automobile company, for example, and posing for drawings as the "grumpy uncle Henrick" in the American Girl "Kit" book.

One day, about three months after I had run my record-setting marathon, I got a call informing me that the company that had made the hit computer game *Myst* was doing a sequel. "There's a role in it for which you'd be ideal," my agent said. "I told them about you, and they'd like an audition tape."

The role, she informed me, was for a character named Gehn, who is the villain of the story and who pops up if you get far enough into the game to find him. The producers had been looking as far afield as New York and Hollywood for a suitable actor but had yet to find anyone who took their fancy. I figured that I had the proverbial snowball's chance in hell, but I let her submit the tape.

A few days later, I was invited to Spokane, Washington, for a more formal audition. Spokane is a fine city—site of the annual Bloomsday Run, which I had done several times—so I happily accepted.

By the time the day was over, the job was mine. Costuming came next, so they sent me to the Seattle Opera Company to be decked out with something suitable for a science-fiction villain. I wound up with boots, a military-looking frock, a scepterlike rod, a meerschaum pipe, and wraparound aviator glasses, all of it much fun.

Filming was in San Francisco. It was all blue-screen work, done in a blue room with a blue door, a blue table, and an apple on a blue pedestal. Blue-screen technology allows the special-effects folks to superimpose whatever they want in the background. Anne was in the control room with the producers, where she could see the lavish, digitally created set in which I was performing. She was particularly impressed by the way that when I picked up the apple, I appeared to be plucking it from a bowl of computer-generated fruit.

After a while, you get a bit punchy doing this, and one day, goofing around between takes, I started singing "O Sole Mio."

"Do it again," someone called from the production booth.

I obliged, and somewhere in the game of *Riven* there is an "Easter egg" (slang for a bonus clip) of Gehn in full operatic voice.

I had always thought *Sweet Charity*, *Sherlock Holmes*, and my days as king of commercials would be the pinnacles of my acting career. But in a totally different way, *Riven* may have surpassed them all. To my amazement, it was the computer-game phenomenon of the year, selling millions of copies and producing an extremely loyal following. Even now, there are Web sites devoted not only to the game but to Gehn, and while I have no idea how to find the Easter egg of me singing in Italian, I'm sure that a little bit of Google searching would reveal the answer.

● ● ●

Working on *Riven* kept me occupied full time for a week. Blue-screen work is difficult because you're interacting with a computer-constructed environment you can't see, and it can require quite a few takes to get it right. "Sorry, we've got to redo that because you just walked through a pillar" is simply part of the process. That meant the hours were long, and for a week I never got to run, though I did get in a few walks.

Normally, that wouldn't have concerned me. The traditional wisdom is that you can miss a week's training and bounce back within a couple of weeks, even if you're bedridden with flu. But I was scheduled to go to Las Vegas immediately after the shoot for a half-marathon, the first in a national series of age-graded races.

I had wanted to do well but expected to be flat and sluggish. Instead, I ran 1:25:24. At age 72, that age-grades to an open-class 1:01:12, only 95 seconds shy of the then-world record. It was also the fastest age-graded masters performance of the year.

• • •

For a year, I thought about Las Vegas and the value of rest. Then I got to talking with my son Philip.

Philip is a water skier, good enough that he was once part of the British national team. It's a sport that requires strength and flexibility as you hit the ramp, leap one hundred feet or more, and land at speeds in excess of 30 miles per hour. Part of his training involved weightlifting—which he worked at even more seriously than I had during my protein-milk-and-egg days in the Catskills.

Serious weightlifters, he said, allow 72 hours' recovery between hard workouts of any given muscle.

I had heard that before but never given it much thought. Like most competitive runners, I followed a hard/easy pattern in which difficult workouts were followed by easy days, allowing 48 hours' recovery. Now, I wondered whether running might be like weightlifting, particularly for senior athletes like me, whose bodies recover more slowly than those of young folks. My experience following the filming of *Riven* seemed to bear this out.

Still, I had never heard of any coach suggesting anything but the hard-easy pattern. Who was I to challenge a protocol accepted by millions of runners? And why modify something that had worked for me so successfully for so many years? I had a nagging fear that if I did, I would lose my competitive edge. Worse, I hated running slowly and always took umbrage at nonrunners who would say, "Oh, so you're a jogger?" I wasn't a jogger, I was a *runner*, and the easiest way to display the difference was to move briskly.

But preserving my image wasn't my primary objective. Nor, for that matter, was accumulating more world records, wonderful as they are. My main goal was simpler: to keep fit as long as I could, even into extreme old age. The best way to do that was to minimize the risk of injury layoffs.

• • •

For two or three months, I continued to procrastinate. Then one day, I ran a brisk, 13-mile training run. It was a good workout, but in the evening I was stiffer than usual, so I bit the bullet and decided that the next day, I wouldn't run, not even slowly. I would walk.

In the morning I was still stiff, so it was easy to stick to the new plan. I lived on top of a hill, so I walked two miles downhill and then back up, averaging about 17 minutes per mile—a brisk walk, but by no means a racer's power walk. In the afternoon, I took a second walk but went only half as far.

The rest did me good, and the next day I felt ready to run. But I was still in the mood to experiment, so (with difficulty) I restrained myself. Again I walked: three miles in the morning and two in the afternoon. By day three, I felt totally loose, free of pain and eager to run, even adding some speed work to it.

The test came in the days after that. Hard-easy pattern said this could be a hard day. My weightlifting-derived formula said to walk again. Did I really want to wait three days? To a nonrunner it may sound odd, but it took an act of courage to take the full 72 hours off: I was *that* fearful that by changing my training, I was discarding everything that had brought me success. But the *Riven* experience had taught me that if I gave myself more rest and stuck to my plans, I would enter my races with fresher legs. Not only would I be running further into old age, but I might be able to race faster than my old training program permitted.

I gave the new regimen a one-month trial. That was all it took to persuade me to stick with it. Because I was also noticing a loss of muscle mass, particularly in my upper body and arms, I decided to add some weightlifting on my off days. The result is a program that looks like a good way to keep running into your seventies, eighties, and (I hope) nineties. With some minor modification to accommodate race schedules, I found that I could run between eight and 16 miles (sometimes with speed work) every third day. On the off days, I walked six miles, usually broken into morning and evening walks ranging from two to four miles. On one walk day I lifted weights with my upper body; on the other, I lifted with the lower body.

It was an intriguing change, not only of pace but of lifestyle. For years, I remained injury free, until I was sidelined for a few months when I broke a kneecap, tripping and falling while warming up my voice to sing the national anthem. In the meantime, I set a lot of records. I might possibly have been faster if I had trained more often . . . but I might also have spent a lot of time on injured reserve. And at 86, I'm still running.

## Still Moving: Cumbria, England

I wandered lonely as a cloud
That floats on high o'er vales and hills,

When all at once I saw a crowd,
A host, of golden daffodils;
Beside the lake, beneath the trees,
Fluttering and dancing in the breeze.

—William Wordsworth

I don't know how many people ever develop philosophies of life, but mine is simple: be kind to everyone, and keep moving.

I like to think both parts are self-evident, but I'm amazed by how many people neglect the latter. Some wind up immobilized by accident or illness, but in old age, it's critical not to allow yourself to become a couch potato by default. Beginning at age 30, the average person loses 1 percent of muscle mass per year from simple atrophy. That adds up to 10 percent per decade—50 percent by age 80—and it's the primary reason people wind up too weak to rise from their chairs without assistance.

The solution is to keep active. In scientific experiments in which frail-seeming seniors are put on weightlifting programs, the results can be remarkable: they regain muscle mass, improve their balance, and become strong enough that often they can dispense with canes and walkers.

When I talk about this, though, people often scoff. "That's easy for you to say," they will respond. "Obviously, you don't have arthritis." But that's not true: I do have some arthritis. It's even in my knees, one of the poorer places for a runner to have it. I'll concede that I'm lucky it's not worse, but joints are like muscles: use 'em or lose 'em. Pain is involved in keeping an arthritic joint mobile, but there is worse pain in not doing it—until eventually you give up and the joint locks forever.

Part of remaining active, therefore, is wanting to do so enough to put up with the discomfort. For me, that's easy. Even if I weren't a competitive runner, I would want to be active. When Anne and I travel, we want to be able to see the sights, and that requires walking, climbing stairs, and otherwise getting out and about. But there is also a need to be psychologically active. When I review my lifelong fascination with old people, I realize that the ones who have always appealed to me are those who remain engaged in life, rather than rooting themselves into routines in which little interesting ever happens. Poets and philosophers have long observed that youth misses so much of what life has to offer because it's too busy doing other things. But old age can have the same effect if it focuses inward on itself. I'm neither a poet nor a philosopher and am long past trying to explain why either of these is the case. Instead, I'm deep into trying to enjoy everything and everyone I meet in my remaining years. The best way to do this, I believe, is by greeting each new year not with dismay but with the childlike expectancy of my favorite question: *what's next?* For me, of course, that often involves running.

• • •

Even though I've been running now for 30 years, it can still surprise me. One of the biggest surprises came on a visit to England, when my son Anthony took me fell running.

I had heard of fell running but never tried it. It's a Scottish and northern English sport that involves running to the tops of big mountains—"fells" in the northern dialect. It was about 18 months after the Twin Cities Marathon, and while I'm always looking for new worlds to conquer, it was Anthony's idea, not mine. He was 52 at the time (I was 73), and he had recently taken a job in the heart of fell-running country in the English county of Cumbria.

Anthony had been running only three years, but he was already a very serious fell runner. Anne and I had been there barely an hour when he offered to introduce me to his new sport. His brother Michael—another relatively recent convert to running—had driven north with us, so the three of us consulted a map, laced up our shoes, and headed out with a hasty and rather vague "be back later" to the rest of the family.

Driving to the start, Anthony took us past vivid-green meadows teeming with sheep and spring lambs. It was a landscape of tidy stone walls separating immaculate farmsteads, a land whose very sight makes one feel cleansed, bodily and spiritually. Then we hit the fells, running up a steep grade of bracken and grass to pleasantly rolling terrain, crystalline air, and vistas that stretched forever.

I was immediately hooked. I had done some cross-country and trail running in the States, but nothing remotely akin to this, which was like a cross between running and orienteering, with the advantage that the northern fell country was cloaked in low, foot-cushioning vegetation that neither blocked the view nor impeded your progress.

The next day, Michael and I bought specialty fell-running shoes that made us feel as though we were running barefoot—but with traction. We practiced a bit on easy hills and then went back out with Anthony on a 23-kilometer challenge that climbed 2,000 feet to an old Roman road on an airy route locally known as High Street.

The view was spectacular, stretching all the way to Scotland. Below was Coniston Water, where in 1967 motorboat racer Donald Campbell died trying to break his own speed record of 276.33 miles per hour. Going faster than 300 miles per hour, his boat hit a wave, went airborne, and dived into the lake, where, 30 years later, his body remained. (It would later be found in 2001.) At least the injuries runners risk pursuing our records have relatively little chance of being fatal—and with my new fell-running shoes, even a sprained ankle seemed unlikely.

Everywhere, the view swept in a 360-degree panorama. I felt on top of the world, literally, emotionally, and spiritually—especially because I was sharing the experience with my sons. Browning was right. If you live with a "what's next?" philosophy, the best really is yet to come.

• • •

Sometimes, though, the "next" isn't quite so pleasant. There were, for example, the two times I dropped out of races.

The first was in the 1997 Houston Marathon, where I was making an attempt to better the time I had posted in my food-poisoning race. On the day before the race, I was doing a slow jog with one of the officials, trying to keep limber without expending too much energy. It was a beautiful day, and I may have commented on it.

"You better enjoy it while it lasts," the official said. "Tomorrow, they're calling for freezing rain."

"No way," I said. It was sunny and 58 degrees—a postcard-perfect day with ideal marathon weather. But the next morning, I woke to snowflakes mixed with rain the temperature of liquid ice. It was worse than any Freeze Y'r Gizzard Blizzard Run. Minnesota can frostbite you without your ever noticing it; this type of cold makes you perfectly aware of every moment's misery. As the race progressed, the day got colder and colder—so cold that when my body started to go numb, my mind went with it. Around me, people were dropping out in droves. At mile seven or eight, the entire Kenyan team packed it in; when I went by, they were boarding a truck, their hyperlean bodies, so well adapted for running in heat, totally unable to cope with these conditions.

With each mile, the field got thinner and thinner, and still I persisted: 10 miles, half-marathon, 15 miles, 30K, and more. By mile 21, I was running virtually alone, fixated on nothing more than covering an additional five miles. Pace didn't matter. There was ice under foot now, I couldn't feel my toes, and my primary concern was not to slip and break a bone. Somewhere in the previous miles, I had discovered that my cap was frozen to my skull. *Odd,* I thought in a mushy sort of way. *Hats aren't supposed to do that.*

I might well have finished the race in this state (or collapsed trying) had a sag wagon not pulled up beside me. "Are you sure you want to keep doing this?" the driver asked. "You don't look too good."

I don't remember what I said, but moments later I was in the van, blessing the heater. I was whisked to the finish, where the medics had set up shop in a convention center, with dozens of blanket-swabbed bundles lying on cots. Periodically, someone would bring me a hot-water bottle, and I would cuddle up with it, dreaming of all those 80-degree races I had hated so much. It was a long time before I ever thought I would be warm again.

The second time that I dropped out of a race was similar. It was the Karrimor International Mountain Marathon, an annual event covering 50 kilometers (or more) in two days—basically fell running with a backpack. It's held in October and the course varies from year to year. Anthony and I had decided to give it a go the fall after he had initiated me into fell running.

Unfortunately, October weather in northern England can be a bit spotty. A major storm hit on race day, obscuring the summits in windy-looking fog. Anthony is a certified mountain guide, so I let him pick our equipment and load our packs with more warm clothing than I really wanted to carry on the run—but then, much of this race was little more than a fast walk. Then our allotted start time came, and we headed out into a wilderness that really was howling.

Not surprisingly, what we found on the first summit was more rain. It was going horizontally toward places we couldn't see, and I had been wrong in my earlier estimation that running involves few life-threatening risks. If you're far enough from civilization and get cold and wet enough, you can die of hypothermia. These were the types of conditions in which that could happen, and because this was a race, we were carrying bare minimum gear, not the type of mountaineering equipment you need to hunker down and wait out a multiday storm. After about seven miles, we had to admit that this was an impossible quest and possibly a dangerous one. We bailed out to the nearest road and went in search of warmth.

But there were still lessons to be gleaned from that day, and I was happy to glean them. One was the amazing degree to which weather can affect your perception of virtually anything. On a good day, fell running is the finest, purest form of running I've ever discovered. On a day like this, it's the finest, purest form of misery. Part of an athlete's "what's next?" attitude must be the willingness to accept misery as one possible answer. The other lesson involved myself. When I was young, I never quit for anything. If I hit a setback, I was always looking for a way around it. New to me in my mid-seventies was the willingness to say "too miserable" and call it a day.

## Turin, Italy—1997

*The Kenyans went by me in a pack, relaxed and elegant, whisking by at about 90 seconds per mile faster than my pace. "Wow," I said to Anthony, who was running with me. "Wouldn't it be wonderful to be able to run with them?"*

• • •

Life has a way of circling back on itself, like a runner on a track, revisiting familiar terrain from an evolving perspective. So it was that in 1997 I wound up back in Italy. Anthony and I were in Turin—birthplace of his mother and residence of the fictional Alvo Berti—pacing each other in the 100th-anniversary running of the Turin Marathon.

In addition to fell running, Anthony was doing marathons, and he had inherited the speed gene, becoming one of the best 50- to 55-year-olds in his club. When the Turin Marathon invited me to its race for an attempt at bettering my own 3:00:58 record, I accepted on the condition that Tony be allowed to run with me and take a shot at beating his own PR of 3:05:40.

It was three months after the filming of *Riven* and my age-graded victory in the Las Vegas International half-marathon, and I had not yet taken the "rest" message to heart. Nine days before Turin, I had run another half-marathon in the same series, and while I had not done as well as in Las Vegas, I was second in the age-graded standings, ahead of such luminaries as Bill Rodgers and Steve Plasencia. As at the Valencia Marathon, I was coming to grips with the fact that on an age-graded basis, I was world-class—by no means an impostor.

At 72 1/2, I didn't have much chance of beating the mark I had set seven months before in Minnesota . . . and I had probably doomed what little hope there was by running an all-out half-marathon so shortly beforehand. But the age-graded races had been the higher priority for me, and it didn't really matter if I was a bit sluggish in Turin because Europe puts aging athletes in a star category unknown in the United States.

Before the race, Anne and I spent several days in the Italian Alps, in Sestriere, a ski town with a network of fine blacktop trails that run all the way to Switzerland and France. One day, I met a man named Giuseppe who had been a fine runner in his youth and still ran almost daily. Over the course of three wonderful days, he introduced me to his own special routes and took me to the local track, which was officially closed but not, he assured me, for us.

I had hoped that Sestriere's seven-thousand-foot elevation might give me a little stamina. Instead it gave me something more important: a calming, spiritual experience that was more than simply a therapeutic recovery from the half-marathon. Jogging in front of corrugated peaks, beneath a sky of finer blue than anything I had seen since my RAF squadron had headed for Africa, I felt like an innocent in a newly created world. With the help of the Alpine scenery, I abandoned any pressure to achieve a record. The race officials told me they would be delighted with whatever result I achieved because I was the oldest record holder ever to enter their race. I would treat the event as a celebration and put on as good a show as I could but not worry about the outcome.

• • •

Part of putting on a good show was allowing a local television station to film my attempt, and in order to keep us from being lost in the pack, the officials had decided to give Anthony and me a 20-minute head start. At a press conference the day before the race, I trotted out my still-good but somewhat rusty Italian, fielding many questions, the most common of which were about whether I thought I could break my own record. My riposte: *Sarebbe un miracolo se lo faccio.* "It will be a miracle if I do it."

The photos and interviews continued at the race start, and the entire town had a festive air, with thousands of spectators, jugglers, musicians, and youths in medieval costumes lining the streets and piazzas. The mayor greeted us and patted us warmly on the back. *In boca lupo*, he said. "In the mouth of a wolf": a traditional good-luck greeting. And then we were off, with all the trappings: a pace car, police car, motorcycle escort, and the television crew that would stay with us the entire way. It was like Valencia, only now I was being cheered in Italian, a language for which I needed no translator, and the weather was a perfect 56 degrees. I might not run another record, but I was going to have a celebration like few others in my life.

The race director was in the pace car, announcing who I was. He was adding something else, but in the carnival atmosphere it was difficult to figure out what it was. Then I got it: *Categoria venti quatro.* He was telling them I had been born in 1924. *A very good year*! I thought.

I found a 6:50 pace and stuck with it for several miles as the course ran through the countryside near Turin. This part of Italy is famous for cherries, and there were orchards in abundance. Then, about halfway through, the Kenyans went by.

The film crew and two motorcycles stayed with me, but the rest of my escort went with the Kenyans. As I watched these perfect runners dwindle in the distance, it crossed my mind that if I were 50 years younger, I might be running with them. I turned that thought over in my mind a few times, but found no regrets. Had I taken up competitive running in my youth, I might well have been among the world's youthful elite. But now, I kept hearing *Eco lo, 'e lui il vecchio, ma credi che ha setantadue anni? Bravo, bravo!* "There he is, it's him, but can you believe he's 72?" Had I begun running earlier, I might now be burned out.

The evening before the race, I chatted with a man in the hotel. He was about Tony's age, slim and athletic looking, speaking heavily accented English and very little Italian. I asked him if he was going to do the marathon and he said no, he was here merely to watch and be part of the race clinic. I introduced myself and asked his name. "Lasse Viren" was the reply.

In much of the 1970s, Lasse Viren was the finest distance runner in the world, collecting four Olympic gold medals. He was the wrong age for me ever to have competed against him, but meeting him made me wonder whether, had I taken up running in my youth, I might have run in the Olympics. It was another intriguing thought, but again there were no regrets. Had I begun running earlier, I would not have had the joy of discovering the sport at age 55. My life would not have been better, merely different.

•  •  •

The kilometers continued to click away. I was enjoying the flat, scenic course, proud to be running with Anthony. He was the picture of a top-class distance runner: five feet nine and lean. He looks a bit like Bill Rodgers and runs with a similar style.

But the day was warming up and my too-recent half-marathon was beginning to take its toll. We slipped from 6:50s to a 7:10, and runners were now catching us in a steady stream. I urged Anthony to leave me and run for his own PR.

The final kilometers brought cobblestoned streets, statues of military heroes on horseback, open-air cafes, church bells, and prettily dressed children accompanying their parents to worship. *Carabiniere* saluted us at every intersection—an acknowledgment more likely aimed at my remaining motorcycle escort than at me. I was fading badly now, but it didn't matter;

the cheers at the end were startling. Finish line spectators had been following my progress on an immense television screen, and I later learned that I had received more coverage than the Kenyans. After the race, it seemed that everyone in the city had seen *l'americano* on TV, and at the finish, they greeted me as Turin's hero of the day.

Joseph Chebet of Kenya won in 2:08:23, followed by two more Kenyans and a young Korean. Anthony ran 3:02:40—a solid PR. My blood sugar plummeted in the final miles, and I finished dizzy and exhausted in 3:20:01, wishing I had eaten more for breakfast as, ironically, another member of the prerace clinic (a young superstar with a 2:07 to his credit) had strongly advised me to do.

At the awards ceremony, I received a spectacular plaque made especially for me. It was a silver rectangle with two gold-colored medals inset on either side, one depicting the ancient Roman walls of the city and the other a map from the 17th century. It was set in a plush black presentation case and is one of my most valued possessions, representing everything I love about Italy.

Two months later, I received my age-group award in the mail. I have an entire roomful of awards, but this one was special. It was tiny—about an inch and a half in diameter—and wafer thin. It bore the marathon logo: a bright red cherry with a single green leaf, embossed on the front in colored enamel, a true work of art. It was made of real gold. In 30 years of running, it is my one and only true gold medal. Will it be my last? Who knows? I am still running, and one of the first things I did when I turned 85 was to start chasing 85–89 age-group records. After that? Well, there's always 90–94.

# ABOUT THE AUTHORS

**John Keston** took up running at 55, rising quickly to the ranks of world-class athletes at distances ranging from the marathon to the mile. He has run with world-class fields in five countries, holds many world, U.S., and British age-group records, and has been inducted into the USA Track & Field Masters Hall of Fame.

He's also spent 60 years as a successful actor and singer, both in Britain and America, and taught classical singing to students who distinguished themselves in Metropolitan Opera auditions. He's had leading tenor roles in grand opera, musical comedy, concert and oratorio, as well as dramatic roles in theatre, film, television, and radio. John was directed by Sir John Gielgud in Noel Coward's *Private Lives*, played the male lead opposite Juliet Prowse in the London production of *Sweet Charity*, and was seen on Broadway in the Royal Shakespeare Company's production of *Sherlock Holmes*. John played Higgins in *My Fair Lady*, Petruchio in *Kiss Me Kate*, and other musical male leads. John toured his one-man show *Expressions of Aging* throughout the United States and England.

He lives with his wife, Anne, in Sunriver, Oregon.

**Richard A. Lovett**, like John Keston, came to running as an adult, when, in his mid-20s, he took up jogging in order to train for a climb of Washington's 14,400-foot Mt. Rainier. Soon, though, he was running races, including 14 marathons and two Ironman triathlons.

A Midwesterner by birth, Rick moved to Oregon, where he coaches Portland's 300-member Team Red Lizard running club. He also coaches private clients, one of whom recently qualified for the 2012 Olympic Team marathon trials.

Rick is also an award-winning science fiction writer, a senior writer for *Running Times*, and a frequent contributor to *Marathon & Beyond*. A former law professor, he also holds a PhD in economics and a BS in astrophysics, which he uses to write science articles for such publications as *National Geographic News*, *Science*, *Nature*, *New Scientist*, and *Cosmos*. He has written more than 3,000 articles and eight books, including two with Olympic coach and marathoner Alberto Salazar. Find him online at *http://running.richardalovett.com*.